Praise for

Kerry Ann Mendez
and
The Budget-Wise Gardener

"Kerry Ann Mendez has revealed the best trade secrets for maximizing your garden budget! *The Budget-Wise Gardener* is full of great strategies to save time while getting the most bang for your buck. This is a must-have resource for practical applications in every outdoor space."

~ Brie Arthur, horticulturist, author of *The Foodscape Revolution*

"Any time I can save money on my gardening obsession I'm happy. But getting the dirt on great garden-related deals from Kerry Ann Mendez will always get my attention. As a talented designer and frugal gardener, Kerry Ann's advice is money in the bank and well worth my time."

~ Joe Lamp'l, founder of joegardener.com and creator/host of "Growing a Greener World" on national PBS

"Whenever Kerry Mendez is at bat I know things are about to get interesting. Kerry is knowledgeable, articulate, and engaging. She delivers fresh, helpful information with brio and class – great stuff that home gardeners and pros alike didn't know they needed to know in order to have better, more sustainable, easier, lovelier gardens. Kerry hits a home run every time."

~ Owen Dell, RLA, ASLA landscape architect, author, educator

"Kerry Ann Mendez is a 'down and dirty' dynamo, connecting with other hands-on gardeners to speak of common bonds and share her considerable know-how."

~ Tovah Martin, author of Tasha Tudor's Garden and many other gardening books

"I am all for saving a little money, but not at the expense of the quality of my flowers and containers. However, it did not take but a few minutes of reading *The Budget-Wise Gardener* to convince me that Kerry Ann 'got it.' Her ideas are simple and down to earth, and make sense horticulturally and financially. I have no doubt that many of them will soon be part of my own garden."

~ Allan M. Armitage, Ph.D., horticulturist, award-winning author,
creator of the app "Armitage's Greatest Garden Plants"

"The topics of Kerry Ann's books are always themed perfectly to our audience at the Boston Flower & Garden Show – in this case, appealing to the thrifty gardener who wants to be the talk of the town without breaking the bank. Kerry Ann's vast plant knowledge and enthusiasm for suggesting just the right plant for every situation make a seat at her lecture and a copy of the accompanying plant list two of the hottest things to score at the show!"

~ Carolyn Weston, Show Director, Boston Flower & Garden Show

"Few people understand how to combine low-maintenance garden design with an abundance of plants, yet Kerry Mendez once again proves that she is master of both. Her indefatigable enthusiasm is evident in her new book, *The Budget-Wise Gardener*, featuring savvy tips for gardeners of all ages, cost-savings ideas for growing a fabulous garden. Astutely practical and sure to inspire."

~ Ellen Ecker Ogden, author of *The Complete Kitchen Garden*

"With her wide experience as home owner, practical gardener, consultant and garden designer, Kerry Mendez understands the many issues facing today's gardeners. Kerry is passionate about motivating people to make the most of their garden, patio or window box – offering excellent ideas and solutions in her approachable no-nonsense books, entertaining lectures and online communications."

~ Adrian Bloom, award-winning designer, writer, nurseryman,
gardener and president of the Blooms of Bressingham Gardens in Norfolk, England

THE
Budget-Wise
GARDENER

THE
Budget-Wise
GARDENER

With Hundreds of Money-Saving Buying & Design Tips
for Planting the Best for Less

Kerry Ann Mendez

st. lynn's
press

PITTSBURGH

The Budget-Wise Gardener
With Hundreds of Money-Saving Buying & Design Tips for Planting the Best for Less

ISBN-13: 978-1-943366-33-0

Library of Congress Control Number: 2017943777
CIP information available upon request

First Edition, 2018

St. Lynn's Press . POB 18680 . Pittsburgh, PA 15236
412.381.9933 . www.stlynnspress.com

Book design – Holly Rosborough
Editor – Catherine Dees

Printed in Canada
On certified FSC recycled paper using soy-based inks

This title and all of St. Lynn's Press books may be purchased for educational, business or sales promotional use. For information please write:
Special Markets Department . St. Lynn's Press . POB 18680 . Pittsburgh, PA 15236

10 9 8 7 6 5 4 3 2 1

TO MY DEARLY LOVED SURROGATE CHILDREN:

Connor Preece

Jill Hendrickson

Gabi Bowditch

Blade and Christina Osborn

TABLE OF CONTENTS

INTRODUCTION

✿

I love getting a deal. And so do you. There is something deeply satisfying when you acquire something highly esteemed for a song. Even better when it's a plant!

✿

I've been called cheap (I prefer frugal) by some in my family. But being thrifty allows me the luxury of splurging at times! Actually, my love of gardening was a direct result of my financial hardships earlier in life. I needed a second job to pay bills, and although I didn't know anything about growing perennials, I applied at a five-acre field-grown garden center.

Getting a tan while I worked seemed like a good idea. Praise the Lord for Melba Higgins who took a risk on me, offered me a job at $6 an hour and mentored me under her horticultural wing.

My budget-wise attitude was put to the test after I became a plantaholic. Flower gardening grew into a passion – and then my livelihood. A home-based gardening business is not a high income profession, yet I was determined to create flower gardens and container gardens that were lush, opulent-looking, and done on a tiny budget. My penny-pinching skills soared to new levels for finding great plants, organic gardening products and other landscaping essentials. I also became skillful at saving money (and time) on routine maintenance chores including watering,

weeding, mulching, preventing critter damage and more. Everything I designed had to be easy on the pocket and on my back.

My most recent book, *The Right-Size Flower Garden*, focused on creating spectacular, non-stop-color gardens that were 50% less work while being environmentally friendly. *The Budget-Wise Gardener* expands on this practicality theme by providing "insider trade secrets" for spending less without compromising quality. You'll learn how to get the best deals by plant group (i.e., perennials, shrubs, annuals); discover sources for amazing finds, including a number that will surprise you; save money on garden and container designs; and spend less time and cash on garden maintenance while embracing sustainable practices.

Sometimes the hunt is more fun than finding the treasure. In this case, however, they are both priceless! Let's enjoy the journey together…

Kerry Ann

HOW TO SCORE GREAT PLANTS FOR LESS...OR FOR FREE!

Welcome to the Academy of Shrewd Plant **Hunters!** Perhaps you're enrolling as a wide-eyed, non-discriminating garden nymph – happy with whatever plant randomly lands in your shopping cart for whatever the price. Or maybe you consider yourself pretty savvy at mining "plant gems" from a quarry of flowering plants. My job as your tutor is to build you into a sophisticated plant geek able to track down elusive deals while getting the highest quality for your money. My mission is to equip you with superior plant scouting skills for capturing the healthiest, best-priced plants and eliminating costly poor decisions. The end goal: heavenly-looking, budget-wise gardens that do not create hell on earth.

The Academy's first course focuses on evaluating contenders for a place in your garden. No more spontaneously reaching for the container with the biggest or most flowers at the garden center. You're going to have cutting-edge assessment tools and precision timing to seize exceptional plants for less. Your untrained eye will develop radar vision. You will quickly identify poorly rooted specimens, pots that have been inconsistently watered and plants on the verge of an insect or fungal outbreak. Your scouting skills will identify prized containers that hold two, three or four closely spaced plants to create an impressive display. Or a hefty two- or three-year-old plant in a one-gallon pot, that will shortly be transplanted to a larger container by nursery staff and priced for twice as much. You will also learn how to "hold your fire" until the sale or clearance price appears. Exciting, heart-pounding stuff!

The following sharp-shooting, purchasing tips are not only about keeping more money in your wallet, you will also receive insightful briefings on how to avoid costly mistakes, such as buying plants with inferior genetics or placing the wrong plant in the wrong spot for the wrong reasons.

As a sophisticated plant geek you will be able to successfully maneuver many different terrains and situations – i.e., garden centers, mail-order catalogs, garage sales, friends bearing plants from their gardens – making informed, money-saving, smarter decisions that will result in luxurious gardens and landscapes.

For practical purposes, I have listed my shopping tips by the following popular plant groups: perennials, biennials, ornamental grasses, bulbs, annuals and flowering shrubs. You'll notice that I left out vegetables, herbs, conifers and trees. That's because my time-tested, tactical training is primarily with ornamentals. However, I do give brief mention to conifers and trees for container planting, in Chapter 4.

But first, before I start pulling designer trade secrets out of my magic garden hat, I want to emphasize that planet-friendly, sustainable gardening practices are of paramount importance. We're making changes to our little piece of the earth. For some gardeners, the biggest challenge to creating a garden of their dreams is to put themselves second and ask: How will it benefit pollinators? Conserve precious water? Keep poisons from entering the ecosystem? And the wonderful news is we can have breathtaking gardens and be good stewards of the planet, by making wise plant choices.

Having said this, it would be a glaring omission for me not to mention neonicotinoids (aka neonics), especially when these are applied to perennials that are nectar and pollen sources for precious pollinators. As you may know, a neonicotinoid is a systemic insecticide that is applied to plants to kill many insects, especially sap-feeding ones like aphids. This poison can also be present in nectar and pollen.

Globe Thistle (Echinops) is a bee buffet!

This is not the platform to get into a long dialog about why I believe these insecticides are dangerous. There is plenty of easily accessible information for you to make your own decision. Rather, for those of you who believe as I do (or you are not sure what you believe), I want to provide a few resources for locating growers, garden centers and mail-order companies that do not use neonicotinoids on their plants.

Neonicotinoid Information Sources

Bee Better. Bee Better's mission is to educate homeowners, community leaders and developers about the importance of sustainable, organic and water-wise garden design, with a focus on native plants for resident and migrating birds, bees and butterflies. The site includes lists of neonicotinoid-free growers, as well as growers that still use neonicotinoids. beebetter.info/

Beyond Pesticides. Features a comprehensive directory of companies and organizations that sell organic seeds and plants to the general public (seeds that have not been coated with bee-harming neonicotinoid pesticides or drenched with them). (beyondpesticides.org/programs/bee-protective-pollinators-and-pesticides/what-can-you-do/pollinator-friendly-seed-directory)

Friends of the Earth. Friends of the Earth works to eliminate pollinator-toxic pesticides like neonicotinoids and glyphosate. They are proponents of organic farming systems that are healthier for bees, butterflies, people and the planet. (foe.org/beeaction/retailers)

North Coast Gardening. Gardening in the Pacific Northwest. This entertaining site offers a wealth of information about plants, garden maintenance, design concepts and gardening tools. It also includes a list of neonic-free growers, seed companies and nurseries (wholesale and retail). (northcoastgardening.com/2015/02/nurseries-neonicotinoid/)

* * *

Now, let's dive into the world of perennials to begin mastering the art of great deals plus smarter plant choices – for maximum color with less work.

Perennials by definition are plants that *should* survive three or more years in their designated hardiness and heat zones. Did you notice that *should* is italicized? That is your first lesson.

There are many factors that can impact a perennial's life expectancy, including a gardener's poor decision making. For example, placing a perennial in too little or too much sun; or planting it too deeply so that soil covers the lower stems; or using a post hole digger to open up a teeny-weeny space in compacted soil, jamming the plant in and expecting it to thrive. If you had trouble working the soil, how do you think those fine little root hairs are going to do?

Self-delusional dreams are also a source of a plant's early demise: "Who cares what the plant tag says concerning sunlight requirements, I want that perennial THERE!" Some folks will go to great lengths for reaffirmation. They'll google dozens of sites until they finally find one that tells them what they want to hear. And zone denial is a killer. Maybe, just maybe, that big ole banana tree will overwinter here in my Maine garden. Dream on! I know. I've done all of the above.

Eye-Spy...

■ **Watch for "recycled" perennials** overwintered from the prior year and returned to spring inventory. Although these plants do not look like the fresh material coming from delivery trucks or production greenhouses, it's what's in the soil that matters. Older plants with more developed root systems will ultimately provide double the plant mass compared to first-year plants in quart or gallon pots.

■ **Do some quick math** in your head (or on your iPhone) to see if it is cheaper in the long run to buy a larger container and then divide it into pieces, versus buying smaller pots priced for less. But a word of warning as you scout the field. There are some perennials that resent being divided (read as *stress out and possibly die*) or have physical root structures that cannot be divided. These include Oriental poppy, baby's breath (Gypsophila *paniculata*), perennial flax (Linum), balloon flower (Platycodon), lupine, Malva, gas plant (Dictamnus), Crambe, butterfly weed (Asclepias) and false lupine (Thermopsis *caroliniana*).

■ **Think spring.** Spring is when some growers will plant multiple small perennial plugs in a one-gallon or larger pot so that it fills in quickly and encourages quick sales. I'm always on the lookout for these remarkable deals. Buy, disassemble and count your booty!

■ **Don't be duped.** Investigate when you see a little plant sitting in the center of a large pot. It may be that the plant was recently transplanted from a smaller container. I'm fine with paying more as long as the perennial is rooted in well. But if it was just transplanted, why pay extra just because of the pot size? If I need more potting soil, I'll buy it! Sometimes you can tell if a plant has been recently transplanted by giving it a GENTLE tug. If it shifts easily in the potting soil, or pops out, you have your answer. Please be kind and leave the plant as you found it (press it back into place). If I really want that particular perennial, I'll go check to see if smaller pots are still available. If not, then why not purchase it later in the season when it's a heftier specimen. I would rather have nursery staff take care of it until it reaches a good size. Then I will whisk it off the shelf, and maybe even divide it into several pieces.

■ **Don't be dirt cheap!** If you want to be astonished by the health and growth rate of your perennials, then invest in healthy soil. There is an age-old worthy saying: *Don't plant a $5 plant in a $1 hole, instead plant a $1 plant in a $5 dollar hole.* Pouring a little love into your soil can transform a spring-planted, 4-inch potted perennial into a hefty gallon-sized specimen later that same season!

■ **Nurture healthy soil.** Healthy soil fosters plants that:
- have more expansive, well-developed roots
- are more drought-tolerant and less stressed by swings in soil temperature
- support lusher top growth (foliage, flowers, fruits)
- are more resistant to disease and insect damage
- are less prone to winterkill

Enrich soil by incorporating organic material into new garden beds or topdressing existing gardens with two or three inches of nutrient-rich matter. Amendments include aged compost, manure, leaf mold and mushroom compost. Check with your regional extension office for locally sourced materials. A complete soil test that includes a nutrient analysis, soil pH and percentage of organic matter is usually around $25, money well spent!

■ **Go for Godzillas.** Save money and planting time by purchasing "Godzilla-size" family members. A super-sized perennial can fill a space that would require multiple smaller-scaled siblings. Here are some ideas:

Average-size	Godzilla-size

Japanese Painted Fern 'Pictum'

Japanese Painted Fern 'Godzilla'

Ligularia 'Desdemona'

Ligularia 'King Kong'

Siberian Bugloss 'Jack Frost'

Siberian Bugloss 'Alexander's Great'

Average-size	Godzilla-size

Black-eyed Susan 'Goldsturm'

Black-eyed Susan *maxima*

Hosta 'Ginko Craig'

Hosta 'Empress Wu'

Little Blue Stem 'Smoke Signal'

Big Blue Stem 'Indian Warrior'

Average-size	Godzilla-size

Coral Bell 'Peach Flambe'

Coral Bell 'Southern Comfort'

Heucherella 'Sunspot'

Heucherella 'Galactica'

Clearance Tables

Clearance tables are a no-brainer for scouting deals. But like milk in a food market, these bargains are typically located at the back of the store. Usually the first perennials to show up in clearance are spring bloomers that are past bloom. What a goldmine! These perennials are relatively fresh – they have not gone through months of stressful living in stuffy pots. The only reason they were relegated to the sale table was because they're flowerless, and garden centers know that most costumers buy plants in bloom. Delaying your purchase saves you 25%, 50% or 75% off the original price! Ephemerals (early spring-blooming perennials that go dormant after flowering) are often quickly marked down, before their foliage starts to look ratty and disappears. But don't be fooled by the shabbiness. Plant them in your garden, mark the location, and they will rise and shine next spring to greet you and early pollinators.

As the season progresses, other perennials will be marked at clearance prices. Again, this is usually because the plant is no longer in bloom. But it may also be that freshly blooming inventory is arriving and space needs to be created. This is good news for shrewd plant hunters!

Given that most plants on clearance racks are not in bloom, and plants tags either don't show a good image or are extremely faded, it can be difficult to decide whether to swoop or skip. That's where my friend Allan Armitage's new app "Armitage's Greatest Garden Plants" comes to the rescue. It has hundreds of plant images and descriptions so you can quickly type in a plant's name and bingo, you have a great photo and helpful growing information.

The "Garden Answers Plant Identification" app is another option. Dave's Garden website also has a plant identification resource: Mystery Plant & Tree ID Forum (davesgarden.com/community/forums/f/plantid/all/).

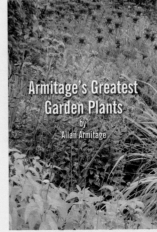

But be aware... I only have a few red flags to wave when it comes to purchasing clearance plants. Of course plants must be healthy. They can't have bugs or disease issues. The potting soil should not be soggy and the plant's crown (where the stems enter the potting medium) shouldn't look dark brown or rotting. There shouldn't be a space between the soil and the pot's edge. This can be caused by inconsistent watering, leading to root stress.

Finally, perennials that have been sitting in their pots for months may have started twirling their "fingers" (I mean roots) in boredom. One sign of a root bound perennial is roots growing through the bottom of the container. Another telltale is when you attempt to slip it out of the pot to plant it in your garden, it doesn't budge an inch. The roots are crammed in the pot. You may have to gently tap on the pot's bottom. If that doesn't work, try banging on it. No? Then put the pot on its side on the ground and step on it, rolling slightly. This adjustment usually does the trick. Sometimes, if I am having a bad day, I'll throw the container to the ground and then step on it. If all of this seems too harsh, then use scissors, a pruning knife or bypass pruners to cut the container open.

The next step is to break apart the dense root mass. If you transplant the perennial as is, you will likely see a dead plant the next season or one that shows little or no growth. Why? Because the roots are coiling around and into themselves. There is no fresh soil with nutrients, water and oxygen to encourage growth. Use a butcher knife, pruning saw or bypass pruner to cut an X into the base. Gently pry the X open to encourage fresh soil to enter this space. Also, rough up the sides of the root ball to loosen and redirect roots into fresh soil. Then place the revitalized plant into fresh soil and water well.

Perennials and shrubs can become root bound when left too long in a pot. Help direct congested roots into fresh soil by slicing an X in the bottom of the root ball and roughing up the sides, freeing roots to seek fresh soil and nutrients.

■ **Should you buy a cultivated variety?** If a perennial is borderline hardy in your area and you're a risk taker, improve the odds of it surviving by buying the species versus a cultivated variety.

Native Purple Coneflower (Echinacea *purpurea*)

Many times the species are hardier due to less meddling with genetics. What do I mean? For example, Echinacea *purpurea*, commonly called purple coneflower, is a wonderful native perennial to North America. Simply stated, Echinacea is the genus name. The next word,

usually lower case and italicized, is the species. And if it is a cultivated variety, or cultivar, then the next word(s) will be capitalized and in single quotations. So Echinacea *purpurea* is a species of coneflower,

Coneflower (Echinacea *purpurea*) 'Hot Lava'

hardy in Zones 3–9. Echinacea *purpurea* 'Hot Lava' is a cultivar, hardy in Zones 5–9. And another tip for increasing the odds of borderline perennials? I've found some white flowering cultivars to be finickier than other colors.

Nativars

This is a good time to bring up nativars. These are cultivated varieties of a native plant. Thankfully, native plant sales are booming, given the heightened interest of incorporating natives, not only to benefit pollinators but also for their less demanding nature. This new interest, along with increased revenue opportunities for those in the industry, has propelled intense breeding within native families to introduce flowers with new colors, sizes, shapes and abundance. And although these nativars may be more striking to consumers, research indicates that many nativars are less attractive, or beneficial, to pollinators. Research is showing that the more a native plant has been "hybridized," i.e., looks different in flower shape or color, the less beneficial it is to pollinators. Annie S. White, at the University of Vermont, under the tutelage of my friend Dr. Leonard

Perry, has been doing extensive field research on natives versus nativars. To learn more about her ongoing work, visit pollinatorgardens.org.

Annie White, conducting research on natives and nativars while a PhD student in Plant & Soil Sciences at the University of Vermont

■ **Pay more, get more?** Sometimes it is wise to pay more money for a larger perennial. There are some perennials that grow very slowly and will not bloom until they reach a certain size and maturity. So while I could save money and buy Dictamnus* in a 4-inch square as a first year specimen, it will most likely take four or five years before flowering. If you are a type-A personality like me, or you're getting up there in years (who isn't?), it just makes sense to spend a few more dollars on an older plant with immediate returns. A few other "tortoise-paced" growing perennials include peony and Baptisia.

Dictamnus is commonly called gas plant because it emits fumes from the flowers that are flammable. Both the foliage and flowers smell like lemon. Please note that resin and oil from the

Gas Plant (Dictamnus *albus*) 'Purpureus'

leaves may cause severe rashes, welts and even oozing blisters. I have not had this reaction, but proceed with caution, especially if you have sensitive skin.

■ **Buy short-lived perennials in 4-inch pots.** Or start them from seed. Why invest money in a large container when the plant will likely fizzle away in three years (maybe less)? Thankfully, most short-lived perennials bloom in their first year. Some attractive "fly-by-nights" include flax (Linum), mullein (Verbascum), Malva 'Zebrina',

Iceland Poppy (Papaver *nudicaule*)

Malva 'Zabrina'

dwarf Delphinium (Delphinium *grandiflorum* and *chinensis*), blackberry lily (Belamacanda), Iceland poppy (Papaver *nudicaule*), columbine (Aquilegia) and English Daisy (Bellis *perennis*). Another dead giveaway that you're looking at a short-lived perennial is when the plant tag states "allow some to reseed to enjoy more the next season."

■ **Buy fast-growing perennials in small containers.** Give these fast growers an inch and they will take a mile – or close to it! Some "fleet of root" include bee balm (Monarda), gooseneck (Lysimachia *clethroides*), obedient plant (Physostegia, and don't be fooled by the cultivar 'Miss Manners'), threadleaf tickseed 'Zagreb' and 'Golden Showers' (Coreopsis), ladybells (Adenorpha) and spotted bellflower 'Cherry Bells' (Campanula *punctata*). Which leads to the question, where are you thinking of planting these? I'm not suggesting that they're bad plants, you just need to be realistic about their intentions. If you think they will politely stay where planted, dream on! Which reminds me, Coreopsis *rosea* 'Dream On' is also aggressive. Fast-spreading perennials usually need yearly "editing" (thinning). Better to plant them where they can run wild and frolic with others of their kind – as a ground cover or in a meadow or wildflower garden.

Spotted Bellflower (Campanula *punctata*) 'Cherry Bells'

Bare Root Plants

Save a wheelbarrow of money by buying daylilies, Hosta and peonies as bare root plants (other perennials are also available). Bare roots cost less to ship than container plants – plus, frequently they have more mature root systems. If you have never planted a bare root perennial, you might feel awkward at first. The "dead looking" root can be unnerving. First, place "sleeping beauty" in some tepid water and allow it to soak for at least thirty minutes to an hour. Then place the hydrated root in a container of potting soil or plant directly in the landscape if the temperature is consistently above freezing.

If you are confused about which end goes up, look closely for stem remnants indicating where the plant was cut back after being harvested the year before. The stem end goes up. Place the bare root in the hole so the crown (where the stem meets the roots) is even with the soil surface. Hold the plant in place with one hand and push soil around the roots with the other, filling the hole. Then water in gently so as not to wash soil away from roots. If you still can't make heads or tails of which end goes up, plant the root on its side and it will solve the problem for you.

A bare root of perennial Russian Sage (Perovskia) being potted up.

After eight weeks the bare root has grown into a gorgeous specimen!

■ **Steer clear of perennials that show signs of insect or disease problems,** no matter how tempting to put them in your cart. Save your Clara Barton skills for your spouse, children, pets or friends. Bringing a sick plant home to the garden is only inviting trouble to spread.

■ **Scrutinize variegated perennials for signs of leaves reverting to solid green.** You really can't blame a plant for trying to shed its variegation. Less chlorophyll (green pigment) in leaves makes a plant less

This variegated Sedum at a garden center is already showing signs of reverting to a solid green.

efficient at photosynthesis, needed for food production. Some variegated perennials that have a tendancy to revert include Sedum, Phlox, Arabis and Heliopsis.

■ **What to do with a lovable "thug":** If you must have a perennial that is considered a thug (a plant that spreads rapidly, invading its neighbors or even your home!) then there are a few options: 1) you can create a meadow garden where it can range freely (assuming it

is NOT on the invasive list, check with your regional extension office); 2) "imprison" it in a large container (with the bottom cut off) sunk into the ground. Make sure the container's sides are at least 6–8 inches long. Or, 3) check if there is a variegated, chartreuse or blue-leaved cultivar in the same family and buy that. As mentioned above, because the leaves contain less chlorophyll, the plant will be less vigorous.

This patch of gold Lily-of-the-Valley (Convallaria *majalis*) 'Fernwood's Golden Slippers' is surrounded by the more aggressive, green-leaved variety.

Shopping for Hosta? 5 Things to Know

Hosta 'Brother Stefan' has deeply puckered leaves. It was the American Hosta Growers Association's 2017 Hosta of the Year.

3. If you see a variegated Hosta with some solid green leaves at its perimeter, choose another plant. It is trying to revert.

4. If you're on the hunt for fragrant flowering Hosta, don't assume the word fragrant on a plant tag means highly scented. It is best to do your own nose test. Most fragrant flowering Hosta bloom in mid- to late summer with flowers that are white or soft lavender.

5. To reduce slug and snail damage, look for Hosta with lots of "quilting" or "puckering" in their leaves. Blue-leaved Hosta are also good choices.

1. Variegated Hosta do not usually develop their mature coloration until three years or older. So the leaf of a first-year Hosta may look very unlike the picture on the plant tag.

2. Solid blue or blue-variegated cultivars may develop green leaves if they've been in too much sun or their leaves have been consistently drenched by overhead watering. The "blue" is actually a wax that can fade away under these conditions. If this happens, don't fret – the blue will return the next season.

Hosta 'Royal Standard' has shimmering white flowers that are prized for their rich fragrance, especially in the evening.

Thyme thrives along this hot, stony outcrop at Coastal Maine Botanical Garden in Booth Bay, Maine.

■ **Looking for drought-tolerant, xeric plants?**
Drought-tolerant, xeric plants are in high demand. When shopping for these, select containers with medium to dry potting soil, NOT soggy soil, which can set back or kill a plant. Inexperienced nursery staff can sometimes overwater xeric perennials, especially when these are mixed in with other inventory. Some xeric perennials include Sedum, hens and chicks (Sempervivum), most silver-foliaged plants, ice plant (Delosperma) and Thyme.

■ **Save money by buying perennials sold as annuals.** Perennials often used in container designs are commonly available in 4-inch pots in the annual inventory. Check for dead nettle (Lamium), creeping Sedum, coral bells (Heuchera), dwarf ornamental grasses, rush (Juncus), creeping yellow Jenny (Lysimachia *nummularia* 'Aurea') and hens and chicks (Sempervivum). There may be other great perennial buys as well. Just remember to keep your hardiness zone in mind as you scan the possible options.

Enjoy Constant Color with Early, Mid- and Late-Blooming Varieties

You can squeeze longer color from a perennial family (genus) by using early, mid- and late-blooming varieties. As one perennial cultivar finishes blooming, the next family member sweeps into action. By the time the latest bloomer crosses the finish line, you may have enjoyed eight or more weeks of constant color! Here are a few perennials that offer early, mid- and late blooming varieties:

ALLIUM

Early: 'Purple Sensation'

Mid: 'Millenial'

Late: 'Medusa'

ASTILBE

Early: 'Fanal'

Mid: 'Bressingham Beauty'

Late: *chinensis* 'Pumila'

DAYLILY

Early: 'Apricot Sparkles'

Mid: 'Barbara Mitchell'

Late: 'El Desperado'

IRIS

Early: Dwarf Crested Iris

Mid: Intermediate Tall Beareded Iris
'Maui Moonlight'

Late: Louisiana Iris
'Black Gamecock' Iris

Two Other Perennial Families that Go the Distance:

PEONY:
Early: Fernleaf Peony *tenuifolia* 'Early Scout'
Mid: Peony Itoh 'Julia Rose'
Late: Peony *lactiflora* 'Esla Sass'

PHLOX:
Early: Phlox *divaricata* 'Louisiana Blue'
Mid: 'Fashionable Early Flamingo'
Late: 'Robert Poore'

31

'Snowcap' covers its tiny frame with masses of flowers.

'Becky' takes the bloom baton and flowers into mid-August. Overlapping with 'Becky' is white coneflower 'Fragrant Angel' (Echinacea) that powers on for a few more weeks. The final athlete in the race is a chrysanthemum 'Daisy White' that crosses the finish line in late fall.

■ **What about coneflowers and coral bells?**
I feel compelled to address these two highly popular perennials that elicit mixed reactions from home gardeners as well as green industry professionals. Many people (including me) believe there has been an excessive number of cultivars released in both genera, resulting in inferior or duplicated plants. So here's the scoop.

'Becky' has extra-stiff, 30"–36" stems that are smothered in large flowers, week after week.

■ **Shasta daisies from June to October.** Sparkling white shasta daisies (Leucanthemum) brighten landscapes and are also great cut flowers. Unfortunately, most only bloom for four or five weeks, even with deadheading. My solution: Dish out 15 weeks or more of "shasta daisies" by using a combination of four different plants. Start with early blooming shastas like 'Snowcap' or 'Snow Lady' that start blooming around mid-June. When these start to sputter out, shasta

Coneflower (Echinacea)

Coneflower *pallida*

Coneflower *paradoxa*

Coneflower 'Cheyenne Spirit'

There are noteworthy coneflowers and there are those that never should have been released to the market. I can't count the number of times I've talked myself into paying a small fortune for a dazzling new coneflower that totally disappeared the next year. I guess that's better than making a rude gesture (a single dead stalk sticking in the air). So what's the deal? Well, for starters, it is usually safer to plant a "straight" species coneflower such as *purpurea, tennesseensis, pallida* and *paradoxa*. The challenge is it's harder to find these, with nurseries filling garden shelves with the newest hybridized fandangos. Thankfully, many garden centers now have dedicated sections for natives. This is where you will typically find these coneflowers.

I'm not suggesting all new cultivars are destined for the compost pile. There are some that are highly praised by green industry professionals for their longevity, strong branching habit and good repeat bloom. A few winners from plant trials include 'Cheyenne Spirit', 'Pica Bella', 'Fatal Attraction' and 'Leilani'. I highly recommend that you check out trial evaluations conducted in your own region. Coneflowers that do great in the Rockies may perform differently than those in the mid-Atlantic. Three trial evaluation sites to check are Colorado State University (https://source.colostate.edu/?s=plant+trial+gardens); Chicago Botanic Gardens (chicagobotanic.org/research/ornamental_plant_research) and Mt. Cuba Center (mtcubacenter.org/research). Mt. Cuba, a botanical garden dedicated to native plants in Northern Delaware, did a study of 48 different coneflowers in 2007-2008 (this is published on their website) and will be launching a new trial in 2018.

A few final remarks about coneflowers – which I do love, really! To thrive, they need full sun and well-drained soil. I find that sparing the fertilizer (organic, of course) produces stronger-stemmed, non-floppy plants. Many green industry professionals recommend removing flowers from newly planted cultivars so the plant's energy is redirected to promote strong root development, rather than to flowers. Some argue that plants should be preened of flowers the entire first season, others suggest only for the first three or four weeks. And if you resent removing the flowers because you think that it's unfair to pollinators, the truth is that many cultivars with unusual flower colors and shapes aren't high, if at all, on pollinators' visitation list.

Coral Bells (Heuchera)

Coral Bell 'Cajun Fire'   Coral Bell 'Spellbound'   Coral Bell 'Sugar Berry'

It seems ages ago when coral bells were primarily admired for their flowers, and leaves were a second thought. Then 'Palace Purple' was named the 1991 Perennial of the Year and the race was on for exotic foliage colors. Similar to the coneflower craze, the cry for the newest and flashiest plants was echoed by consumers, as well as by income-driven growers. Many good plants were introduced as a result, and some real duds.

It's fair to say that most coral bells look irresistible as first-year plants on nursery shelves. Sadly, their true colors don't show until the second or third year when genetics start telling the real story.

In addition to genetic makeup, the species of coral bells (there are over 80) can play a big part in how it will perform in your garden. Eastern species, like villosa and americana, accept heat and humidity much better than Western ones. And those with micrantha in their "blood" are generally not as cold tolerant.

One way to eliminate trial and error and save yourself frustration and money is to check out Heuchera trial evaluations for your climate and zone. For example,

Mt. Cuba Center (in Hockessin, DE) conducted a trial on 83 different cultivars in two species, villosa and americana, from 2012-2014. The top ten performers were 'Citronelle', 'Bronze Wave', 'Cajun Fire', 'Color Dream', 'Steel City', 'Caramel', 'Apple Crisp', 'Frosted Violet', 'Southern Comfort' and 'Spellbound'. Chicago Botanic Garden and Colorado State University have also conducted and published studies.

Gardeners also play a part in a coral bells' destiny. They require good drainage and air circulation; they hate wet soil – they're not water plants or fire hydrants. In colder climates, do not plant coral bells where snow crashes off a sloping roof or piles up from snow blowers and plows. Large piles are slow to melt in spring, keeping the soil cold and wet for much longer (which is bad as well for any perennial that demands sharp drainage). Gardeners also need to watch for heaving plants in spring. As coral bells age, their crowns are prone to rising above the soil surface, exposing roots – especially common in colder climates where soil freezes and thaws. Gently press these insurgents back down into the ground.

BIENNIALS

The rich purple domes of Angelica *gigas* partner nicely with light pink Japanese Anemone

Gloriosa Daisy

Biennials can be maddening for some gardeners: they are experts at hide and seek. To appreciate biennials you need to know their modus operandi. Simply put, in the first year they only produce foliage, in the second year flowers appear, and by the third year the party is over. The plant is dead. BUT…there *should* be (did you catch the italics?) little seedlings scattered about the garden for you to find. As they mature, this will count as year one and the story continues. Some biennials are rapid reseeders, like forget-me-nots. Others, not so much, like Angelica *gigas*.

Some commonly sold biennials include foxglove (Digitalis), hollyhock (Alcea *rosea*), wallflower (Cheiranthus), dame's rocket (Hesperis), sweet William (Dianthus *barbatus*) and Canterbury bells (Campanula *medium*). And to make matters more confusing, some short-lived perennials are grouped with biennials. These include columbine (Aquilegia), Iceland poppy (Papaver *nudicale*), Miss Willmott's ghost (Eryngium *giganteum*), gloriosa daisy (Rudbeckia *hirta*), English button daisy (Bellis *perennis*), rose campion (Lychnis *coronaria*) and lupine.

Sea Holly (Eryngium) 'Miss Willmott's Ghost'

Russian Hollyhock (Alcea *rugosa*)

Now, on to money-saving, smart purchasing tips for biennials:

■ **Consider buying seeds.** Many biennials are sold as seeds, which is the least expensive way to purchase them.

■ **Buy first-year plants in small pots or when they go on sale.** To save additional money, purchase pots in fall when prices have been slashed. Then set the first-years out in the garden where you want to see flowers the next season.

■ **Avoid buying second-years.** Don't waste your money on second-years that have been marked down for sale, unless there are still a few flowers/seed heads left to salvage. I still wouldn't bite unless the plant was marked at least 75% off and I was in a risk-taking mood.

■ **Create a bloom cycle.** Prime the garden pump and buy one first-year plant in a small container and one second-year plant in bud or just starting to bloom (usually sold in quart or gallon pot). This way you have a complete cycle already in place in the garden.

■ **Hollyhocks and rust.** Hollyhocks are beloved as old-fashioned cottage flowers. But they are prone to getting rust, a fungal disease on their leaves that is very hard to treat. Thankfully, fig-leaf (Alcea *ficifolia*) and Russian (Alcea *rugosa*) hollyhocks are more resistant to rust and can be longer-lived as well.

■ **Dazzled by Gloriosa Daisies?** Eye-popping varieties of Gloriosa Daisy (Rudbeckia *hirta*) like 'Cherry Brandy', sell like hotcakes when in bloom. They are usually sold in gallon-sized containers in the perennial section and cost a pretty penny. Remember, this beauty will most likely be dead the following year. I'm not saying that you shouldn't make impulse buys, just be an informed consumer, and allow some to reseed. FYI: most Rudbeckia with fuzzy leaves like 'Cherry Brandy' are considered short-lived perennials or biennials.

■ **Carrots in flower...double the pleasure.** You might be surprised to learn that carrots are biennials. If you have traditionally grown these for their yummy roots, why not leave a few unharvested for flowers next year. They have striking Queen Anne's lace-like flowers all summer long.

Gloriosa Daisy (Rudbeckia *hirta*) 'Cherry Brandy'

Biennials aren't no-brainer plants. They take some planning. If you want to save money and the headache of making sure that 1) second-year plants successfully reseed, 2) you don't weed seedlings out as they emerge, and 3) the seeds land where you actually want flowers, then purchase **long-lived perennial lookalikes** instead. Here are a few captivating substitutes to consider:

4 Long-lived Perennial Lookalikes

BIENNIAL

Foxglove (Digitalis)
Miss Willmott's Ghost (Eryngium)
Sweet William (Dianthus barbatus)
Lupine (i.e. Russell Hybrids, Popsicle series)

Sweet William
(Dianthus *barbatus*)

Sundial Lupine
(Lupine *perennis*)

PERENNIAL

Digitalis *grandiflora* (also known as *ambigua*)
Eryngium 'Big Blue'
Dianthus *barbatus* 'Heart Attack'
Lupine *perennis*

Foxglove
(Digitalis *grandiflora*)

Sea Holly (Eryngium)
'Big Blue'

ORNAMENTAL GRASSES

Ornamental grasses rock! They have many "plant-and-forget" attributes. Most grasses are drought tolerant, deer and rabbit resistant, pollinator friendly, offer long seasonal interest, require no fertilizer, and are pest and disease free.

But to get the most bang for your buck from these superstars, I recommend considering the following characteristics before purchasing:

A Grass's Posture

Is it narrow and upright like native feather reed grass 'Karl Foerster' (Calamagrostis *acutiflora*) or does it have a wide, arching habit like Miscanthus *sinensis* 'Morning Light'? Maybe it's short in stature with cascading blades like hakone grass (Hakonechloa *macra* 'Aureola'). Perhaps it has more of a spikey, tufted shape like blue fescue 'Elijah Blue' (Festuca *glauca*), while fountain grass 'Desert Plains' (Pennisetum *alopecuroides*) has a mounded appearance. Before snatching a grass off the shelf, you need to make sure the space you have for it will flatter its physique. The last thing you want to do is cram ornamental grasses together or site them where they'll be a nuisance, like putting wide-growing Miscanthus 'Gracillimus' alongside a narrow pathway where its wide, sharp-edged blades "greet" passersby.

Feather Reed Grass (Calamagrostis *acutiflora*)

Hakone Grass (Hakonechloa *macra*) 'Nicolas'

Pennisetum *alopecuriodes* PRAIRIE WINDS 'Desert Plains'

Miscanthus *sinensis* 'Morning Light'

A Grass's Temperature Range

Grasses are categorized as cool or warm season grasses.

Cool season grasses are quick to wake up and break dormancy in spring. The cold soil temperature doesn't faze them. They prefer cooler air temperatures as well and may start to go dormant or look shabby in high heat and extended drought, making them better choices for cooler zones. Most are short in stature, under four feet tall, and flower early, by June. Cool season grasses are generally evergreen and benefit from frequent dividing, unlike their warm season cousins. Given that cool season grasses show up early to work, they are lovely planted with spring blooming bulbs to screen ripening foliage, but they also make great dance partners for later bloomers like Alliums.

Cool season grass, Nassella, creates a magical scene in Chanticleer's gravel garden in late June.

Warm season grasses are crowd-stopping showoffs. Although pokey to get going in spring, they hit a major growth spurt come summer. Flowering starts in summer, with most peaking in fall. Warm season grasses can get huge, some reaching 15 feet. Their tallness makes them ideal for mid- to back border planting, which also solves the problem of hiding their ugly, slow-to-green-up appearance in spring. If winter landscape beautification is your goal, then warm season grasses are your answer (although Calamagrostis, a cool season grass, is also spectacular).

Blue Switch Grass (Panicum *virgatum*) 'Prairie Sky'

Little Bluestem (Schizachyrium *scoparium*) 'Smoke Signal'

Blue Grama Grass (Bouteloua *graciles*) 'Blonde Ambition'

Prairie Dropseed (Sporobolus *heterolepis*)

Tortoise or hare? Is the grass a well-behaved, clump-forming variety or does it run like a world class sprinter? Knowing its inclination is essential for your garden sanity. Clump formers slowly get bigger around their "waistline" while runners seem to take off even before you finish planting them. A rapidly spreading grass can make a good groundcover but it will not make a polite guest in a more structured gathering. Yes, you can imprison the speedster in a container as mentioned earlier, but its stoloniferous or rhizomatous roots can be wickedly clever at finding an escape route. Two grasses that regularly break the speed limit are ribbon grass (Phalaris *arundinacea*) and blue lyme grass (Elymus *arenarius*). Of course, those listed on your region's invasive list are out of question.

Ribbon Grass (Phalaris *arundinacea*)

Indian Grass (Sorghastrum *nutans*) 'Sioux Blue'

■ **Save money on winter birdseed** by planting ornamental grasses with seed heads that feed hungry birds. Good native grass choices include little bluestem (Schizachyrium *scoparium*), prairie dropseed (Sporobolus *heterolepis*), switch grass (Panicum *virgatum*), big bluestem (Andropogon) and Indian grass (Sorghastrum).
■ **Control erosion with native, drought-tolerant ornamental grasses.** In addition to having dense, matted root systems, the foliage mitigates downpours from washing soil away – plus, the seed heads attract birds. Here are

a few winners: prairie dropseed (Sporobolus *heterolepsis*), Sideoats grama (Bouteloua *curtipendula*), Indian grass (Sorghastrum), little bluestem (Schizachyrium *scoparium*) and switch grass (Panicum *virgatum*). Two other workhorses (although technically not grasses) are Appalachian sedge (Carex *appalachica*) and Pennsylvanian sedge (Carex *pensylvanica*).

■ **Be aware of heavy reseeders.** Heavily reseeding grasses can wear on one's patience. Think dandelions. A few progeny are okay; hundreds, not so much. Some grasses that can be overly enthusiastic include northern sea oats (Chasmanthium *latifolium*), Miscanthus *sinensis* and some fountain grasses (Pennisetum). Not surprising, prairie grasses like little bluestem and Indian Grass also reseed. NOTE: Miscanthus *sinensis* is listed as invasive in over 20 states. Chicago Botanic Garden researched Miscanthus *sinensis*' viability and discovered seed production per plant ranged anywhere from 497-seed ('Dixieland') to 349,327-seed ('Keline Silberspinne'). Those that had no viable seeds were 'Hino', 'Silberpfell', 'Cabaret' and Miscanthus x *giganteus*.

Miscanthus *sinensis* var. *condensatus* 'Cabaret'

■ **Some warm season grasses need cutting back in fall, before the snows arrive.** As mentioned earlier, most warm season grasses are valued for winter interest. But if you live in a region with heavy snowfall, some warm season grasses are best cut back in fall, due to less sturdy stems that collapse under snow and ice. If these are not cleaned up in fall, it can be tedious to remove wet, packed-down blades in spring. Grasses that may benefit from a fall shearing include pink muhly grass (Muhlenbergia), fountain grasses (Pennisetum), moor grass (Molinia) and frost grass (Spodiopogon *sibiricus*).

■ **A Hakone grass that sweeps in one direction.** Hakone grass 'Aureola' (Hakonechloa *macra*) has an unusual growth habit in that its blades tend to sweep in one direction, versus splaying in all directions like other hakone grasses. This one-sided habit can be useful in containers as well as along sidewalks and over retaining walls.

Hakone Grass (Hakonechloa *macra*) 'Aureola's blades all cascade in the same direction

The American Horse sculpture in a meadow at Frederik Meijer Gardens and Sculpture Park.

■ **Save money, buy grasses as plugs.** It can get pricey to fill a large area with graceful, clump-forming ornamental grasses. Depending on your budget and level of patience, buy grasses as plugs versus in large containers. First, ask your local garden center if they can order plug trays for you from their wholesale sources. If that isn't an option, then check into great mail-order companies like Bluestone Perennials (bluestoneperennials.com), American Meadows (americanmeadows.com) or Prairie Moon Nursery (prairiemoon.com) that offer 3-inch and up pot sizes with volume discounts. You could also buy large containers at garden centers and divide them. But before going this route, be sure to eat your Wheaties. Large ornamental grasses can be a bear to divide. Recommended tools include a butcher knife, Sawzall, miniature chainsaw, machete or axe. Be sure to rope off the area from pedestrian traffic.

■ **Don't count on a peek-proof privacy screen.** Ornamental grasses are often used as privacy screens or to block unsightly views. But remember, even if you combine warm and cool season grasses for maximum shielding, there are always "peek-a-boo" months in early to mid-spring when nothing stops the eye.

BULBS AND CORMS

Species Tulip *wittallii*

A display of magnificent tulips is heart-stopping when in bloom. The same can be said when they all disappear a few years later. Sadly, the majority of new cultivars are not long-lived, even less so where gnawing deer or rabbit exist. Thankfully, there are tulips that buck the trend and save you money. In addition to being low on the critter browse list, species bulbs can live for years and even multiply. Species tulips have small flowers with a rich assortment of colors. They vary in height from 4 to16 inches with hardiness zones ranging from 4 to 7. Species tulips tend to bloom earlier than their big brothers.

Allium 'Mt Everest'

Summer Snowflake (Leucojum *aestivum*)

Winter Aconite (Eranthis *hyemalis*)

Snowdrops (Galanthus *nivalis*)

Spring blooming bulbs that are *usually* (there is that italicized word again!) snubbed by deer and rabbits include: Allium, species tulips, Camassia, Hyacinth, Fritillaria, snowdrops (Galanthus), snowflakes (Leucojum), winter aconite (Eranthus) and blue squill (Scilla). Daffodils (Narcissus) are ignored by ALL furry critters, given that the bulbs are poisonous.

Checkered Lilies (Fritillaria *meleagris*)

Tulip 'Candy Club'

numerous flowers per stem. Some outstanding mail-order companies for bulbs include Brent and Becky's Bulbs (NC), John Scheepers (CT), Van Engelens (CT) and ColorBlends (CT).

■ **Protect bulbs from voles (nasty, nibbling field mice).** Voles can be tremendously destructive - not only to bulbs but also to perennials, shrubs and trees. Some bulbs, like daffodil, Colchicum and Hyacinth, are poisonous and require no protection. But most bulbs are fair game. Simple, inexpensive defense shields to protect bulbs include chicken or turkey grit (available at farm and feed stores), crushed gravel or sea shells. When placed in planting holes, these sharp-edged elements make quite an impression on tender noses.

■ **Think outside the bulb box.** As an alternative to planting organized groups of bulbs, why not design floral arrangements? Pick three or four bulb varieties that bloom at or around the same time. Consider flower color and stem height as you contemplate your design. Then plant the bulbs in the ground as if you were placing

Daffodil (Narcissus) 'Thalia'

■ **Two for the price of one!** Many spring blooming bulbs only produce one flower per bulb or stem. Maximize color by planting these tulips that produce multiple flowers on each stem: T. *praestans* 'Unicum' (red); T. *praestens* 'Fusilier' (red), T. 'Antoinette' (soft pink, cream and green) and others known as tall bunch flowering tulips. Daffodils in the Jonquilla, Triandrus and Tazetta divisions (there are 12 divisions based on flower form) also bear

stems in a vase. I find it easiest to dig one large hole, set the bulbs in place, toss crushed gravel (or other sharp fragments) over the bulbs, and shovel soil on top of the arrangement. What a thrill to see your artwork greet you in spring!

■ **Restrain yourself.** Wait until bulb prices are slashed by 50% or more before putting your money down. If you're worried that there won't be enough time to plant these before the ground freezes, relax. I've got your back, and a bulb auger. Bulb augers are sold at garden centers and on line. They attach to electric or battery-powered drills and make planting bulbs of all sizes a cinch and fun!

■ **Buy bulbs in bulk quantities.** This can save a lot of money, as well as shipping costs if ordering online. Bulk orders can range from 25, 50, 100 or 500 bulbs. Share the order with friends. You may even save enough money to pay someone to plant them for you.

■ **Cut out the middle man!** Instead of buying the following perennials in containers, purchase them as corms or tubers and save at least 75% or more. Popular perennials that you can easily start yourself are montbretia (Crocosmia), blazing star, also called gayfeather (Liatris), foxtail lily (Eremurus) and blackberry lily (Belamcanda).

Foxtail Lily (Eremurus) 'White Beauty'

Blackberry Lily (Belamcanda) 'Freckle Face'

Lilium bulbs: another cut-out-the-middle-man group

Lilium bulbs are effortless to start. Just dig a hole as you would for a spring blooming bulb, drop in the bulb, toss in crushed gravel, push back soil, press down. Bingo! These can also be purchased in bulk quantities to save even more money.

Treat yourself to months of heavenly blooms by combining different lilium species. The earliest to pop open in June are Asiatic lilies (most are not fragrant), then Martagon lilies; followed by Trumpets (fragrant), Orienpets (fragrant) that overlap with Orientals (fragrant) and wrapping up in early September with Lilium *speciosum* var. 'Album' and *speciosum* var. 'Rubrum' (fragrant). All of these can be purchased online.

Lilium *speciosum rubrum*

Asiatic Lily 'Cappucino'

Oriental Lily 'Muscadet'

Trumpet Lily 'Pink Perfection'

Orienpet Lily 'Satisfaction'

Martagon Lily 'Sunny Morning'

■ **Plant taller flowering bulbs in back, little ones up front.** Stop being unnerved by messy, slow ripening leaves of spring blooming bulbs. Solve the problem by planting taller flowering bulbs (with larger leaves) in the back of the garden so that their wardrobe change is less noticeable. Plant miniature bulbs in the front and mid-border; these refined beauties still offer a splash of welcomed color, but their foliage ripens quickly, making a timely exit.

■ **Some Alliums I don't invite to the party.** Alliums are extremely popular. Rightly so, given they are drought and critter resistant; tolerate a range of soil conditions; vary in height from three inches to four feet (or taller); range in color from blue, purple, white, pink and yellow;

Allium 'Hair'

Purple Allium and gold Spirea

and sport striking oval, spherical or globular flowers that are pollinator buffets. Having said this, there are some varieties I would never invite back into my bed. They seeded far too aggressively and became a nightmare. Some "fertile myrtles" in my gardens include Allium *azureum* (blue allium), A. *sphaerocephalon* (drumstick allium), and A. 'Hair' (allium having a bad hair day). I also found Allium a. 'Purple Sensation' to be on the verge of annoying. Not only because it would seed around, but its huge, strappy leaves begin to get ugly (go dormant) just as the Allium enters peak bloom.

■ **Bouquets for giving.** Present friends and loved ones with a bouquet of colorful flowering bulbs in a pretty container. What a unique, inexpensive gift that will be enjoyed for years! Order spring, summer or fall blooming bulbs in fall, plant in recycled plastic nursery pots, and then "plant" the pots in your flower garden, vegetable bed or compost pile for the winter. Note: this only works in Zones 7 or colder. Cover the pot with a piece of chicken wire or hardware cloth to keep critters from digging up and devouring your gift. The bulbs should emerge and go into bloom the next year at their scheduled time. Just before presenting the gift, lift the nursery pot from the ground, set it in a decorative container, tie with ribbon and TA-DA, you have made someone's day! When picking bulbs for your bouquet, keep flowering heights under 3 feet for best results.

Colchicum

■ **X marks the spot!** Eliminate costly mistakes. How many times have you sliced into a hidden bulb or late-emerging perennial while digging in another plant? Heartbreaking. Save yourself the agony by marking the spots with attractive foliage of spring or fall blooming bulbs. Colchicum and Lycoris are fall blooming bulbs with foliage that appears in spring, then goes dormant in summer, before leafless flowers pop

Naked ladies (Lycoris *radiata*)

up in autumn. Grape hyacinth (Muscari) flowers in spring, goes dormant and then fresh foliage sprouts in fall.

■ **A simple way to eliminate rotting.** Some flowering bulbs are prone to rotting due to their unusual bulb shape. Crown Imperial (Fritillaria *imperialis*) is one. It has a divot in the bulb from which stems emerges. The depression can capture water and cause rot. This exotic looking perennial bulb will cause heads to turn at its brilliantly colored flowers, as well as noses to wrinkle at its skunky smell. This is not a plant for entranceways or entertainment areas. Tuberous Begonia is another bulb with a depression in its top. Even though it is considered a throwaway annual by many, it can be easily overwintered to replant year after year. Instead of planting both bulbs with the cavities facing upward (as the labels instruct), plant bulbs on their **side**, eliminating rotting. The emerging stems will quickly readjust themselves to grow skyward.

Imperial Lily (Fritillaria *imperialis*)

ANNUALS

Cosmos

Growing annuals from seed is the least expensive route. Some varieties need to be started indoors before the little darlings can be transplanted outside. Gardeners who choose this scenario have the time, temperament and space. I strike out on all three! That is why I look for annuals that can be directly sown into my garden after the danger of frost. Plus, I save money on potting soil and containers. Annuals that can be seeded this way include cosmos, zinnia, marigold, cleome, baby's breath, sweet alyssum, California poppy (Eschscholzia *californica*), red Flanders poppy, Melampodium, nasturtium and sunflowers. Some annuals can also be directly sown in fall to bloom the following year. Not surprising, some of these – like cosmos, larkspur, love-in-a-mist, Bidens and pansies – happily self-sow all on their own from existing plants. Many biennials can also be seeded in fall, including foxglove, Siberian wallflower (Chieranthus), sweet William and hollyhock.

Red Poppy (Papaver *rhoeas*)

Zinnia

Nasturtium

California Poppy (Eschscholzia *californica*)

■ **Save a lot with quantity purchases.** Annuals in containers are usually sold in 3-, 4- or 6-inch squares and rounds; 4- or 6-cell packs; or in flats. The number of plants per flat varies (from 16 to 48) based on the size of the container or cell. The more plants you buy, the more you save. You can save up to 20% (or more) if you purchase a flat versus individual containers. If you don't need all of the plants, share some with friends. If purchasing annuals in cell packs, look for packs with deeper cells, i.e. 3 inches or more. This promotes better root development, reduces transplant shock and jump-starts an annual's performance after transplanting. Plus, be sure each cell contains an annual!

■ **Watch for hanging baskets and mixed containers recently put on sale.** Often it is much cheaper to buy these, disassemble the inventory, and reuse as needed. Sometimes this is the only way to acquire annuals that have already sold out in smaller containers.

■ **What you should know about stem cuttings.** Stem cuttings are an easy way to save, big time! I prefer the simplest technique – rooting them in plain ole water. Annuals that can be propagated this way include coleus, Torenia, annual geraniums, sweet potato vine and petunias. But don't stop at this list. Experiment with some of your favorite annuals. You can take cuttings at any time, but if done in spring, you'll have many little clones to plant in your garden in a month. Take a sharp pair of scissors and cut a 3 to 4-inch stem from "momma."

A tray of stem cuttings at Frederik Meijer Gardens and Sculpture Park

Make sure the cut is just above where a leaf (or pair of leaves) intersects the stem. Strip off the leaf (leaves) just below the cut. This part of the stem will be submerged in water. Remove any flowers or buds on the stem. If the leaves are large, cut some in half to reduce transpiration. Then place the stem in a glass or small jar and fill with water so the water line is just below the first set of remaining leaves. At least 1/3 of the stem cutting should be above the container's rim. Depending on the size of the container, multiple cuttings can be placed in it. Set the cloning factory in a bright window (not direct sun) and smile, thinking of all the money you will be saving! It is important to change the water each day so bacteria doesn't build up, leading to stem rot. Use room temperature water. Once the cuttings develop roots about 1/2 inch in length, transplant them to small pots (or cells) filled with quality potting soil. Continue to grow in pots for a few weeks until a gentle tug on the stem is met with resistance, indicating a nice root structure. Then take them out into the big wide world and plant away (assuming there is no longer any danger of frost).

Snapdragon

■ **Some annuals come back for an encore!** A number of annuals actually behave like short-lived perennials, returning for two or three years. Don't throw them in the compost pile. It is very likely they will greet you the following spring. If these are planted in a container, relocate it to an unheated garage or shed. "Hardy" annuals include Dianthus, snapdragon (Antirrhinum), Portulaca, 'Black and Blue' Salvia and dusty miller (Senecio *cineraria*).

■ **Watch for June sales.** These can be a real bonanza, especially if you can delay planting some garden beds or containers until the price slashing begins. Even though inventory may look a bit tired, most plants will bounce back after old growth is sheared and organic liquid fertilizer, like Neptune's Harvest, is applied. These reinforcements can also replace cool season annuals that are starting to falter from rising temperatures.

■ **Drop and go.** Sometimes I just don't have the time, creativity or interest to assemble a traffic-stopping container. Thankfully others do, especially at garden centers. I'll shop for a gorgeous combo hanging basket that complements a container I need to fill, purchase the basket (hopefully on sale), drop it in my container, remove the plastic arms and admire my work.

■ **Checklist for the clearance table.** Scan clearance annuals for those that, 1) act like short-lived perennials, 2) easily reseed from faded flowers, 3) can be grown as houseplants or 4) can be overwintered in a dormant state.

Salvia *guaranitica* 'Black and Blue'

Houseplants with handsome leaves make great "annuals"

Houseplants can be appreciated year-round, inside and out. They are usually much less expensive than seasonally displayed tropicals that are valued for their foliar appeal (and then typically tossed at the end of the season). Houseplants to check out include Croton, 'Rita's Gold' fern (Nephrolepis *exaltata*), aluminum plant (Pilea *cadierci*), wandering Jew (Tradescantia *zabrina*), rex Begonia, blushing bromeliad (Neoregelia *carolinae* 'Tricolor'), prayer plant (Maranta *leuconeura*), mosaic plant (Fittonia), ti plant (Cordyline *fruticose*), Calathea, ZZ plant (Zamioculcas *zamiifolia*), Gardenia, purple passion plant (Gynura *aurantiaca*) and spider plant.

Ti Plant (Cordyline *fruticose*)

A lovely container created with mostly houseplants, designed by Deborah Trickett, owner of
The Captured Garden

Croton

Mosaic Plant (Fittonia)

Prayer Plant (Maranta *leuconeura*)

■ **Annuals that double as houseplants provide twice the value.** Some annuals in the garden can double as winter houseplants – a valuable attribute. Instead of throwing annuals in the compost pile in fall, transplant these "snowbirds" to decorative containers and bring them inside to warmer weather. Be sure to first check leaves for any stowaway bugs. Annuals that can switch-hit include New Guinea Impatiens, coleus, potato vine, Lantana, Heliotrope, Moses-in-a-basket (Tradescantia *spathacea*), Plectrantus 'Mona Lavender', Alternanthera 'Partytime', and geranium (Pelargonium). Geranium 'Persian Queen' has dazzling yellow leaves with hot pink flowers. It's best viewed with sunglasses.

Geranium 'Persian Queen'

■ **Some annuals can be overwintered in a dormant state.** Place these in a cool, dark location like a basement, unheated sunporch, garage or even an attic. Cut back foliage of potted plants and water once before putting into seclusion. Geranium, Agapanthus and some tropicals are good candidates. Some annuals, like geranium and rex Begonia, can be overwintered without any soil. Just hang their roots upside down in a cool, low-lit spot with good air circulation.

■ **Put heavy reseeders to good use.** Some heavily reseeding annuals can outstay their welcome. Instead of banning these from the garden, why not take advantage of their prolific nature and plant them in a meadow or wildflower garden? Some possible candidates

In the fall I potted this Coleus from my garden and brought it inside as a houseplant. That was two years ago!

Tropical Milkweed (Asclepias *curassavica*)

Save money with annuals that grow by leaps and bounds! Put more money back in your pocket by planting wide spreading annuals. As quasi ground covers, each plant can sweep over three or more square feet. These can also be very effective as solo plantings in containers or hanging baskets. Some swarming annuals include Supertunia Vista petunias, Tidal Wave petunias, Superbena Verbenas, potato vine, fan flower (Scaevola), licorice plant (Helichrysum), Dichondra 'Silver Falls' and Torenia 'Midnight Blue'.

include Verbena *bonariensis*, cornflower 'Blue Boy' (Centaurea *cyanus*), feverfew (Tanacetum *parthenium*), plains Coreopsis (Coreopsis *tinctoria*), dwarf larkspur (Delphinium *tricorne*), Nicotiana, blood flower (Asclepias *curassavica*), Nigella and Alyssum. These and other contenders are usually found in wildflower seed mixes.

Conserve water and time with highly drought tolerant annuals. Sun lovers include Lantana, moss rose (Portulaca), Cosmos, marigold, globe amaranth (Gomphrena), Celosia, Zinnia (Profusion series) and dusty miller (Centaurea *cineraria*). Shade equivalents include wax and dragon wing Begonia, Alternanthera and Browallia.

Fan Flower (Scaevola) 'Whirlwind'

FLOWERING SHRUBS

Flowering shrubs are my new superhero plants. They rescue me from tedious maintenance – and they are drop-dead gorgeous. They provide everything I wish for and I give nothing (or little) in return. If I weren't talking about plants, I would sound severely dysfunctional. Perennials used to own my heart, but now they're slowly being replaced with dazzling shrubs. I will always embrace high-performing perennials in my beds, just not as many.

Abelia c. 'Ruby Anniversary' backdropped by panicle Hydrangea

Bare Root: trim the fat and save a bundle!

Flowering shrubs are sold three ways: in containers, as ball and burlap specimens (B&B), or bare root. The least expensive option is bare root. Dormant shrubs are harvested from the ground, soil is washed from the roots, and then plants are shipped in spring for immediate planting. Bare root shrubs are commonly available by mail order. Planted correctly, bare root shrubs typically go through less transplant shock and establish more quickly than container or B&B plants. They are also much lighter and easier to work with. The key is proper planting. This isn't hard, you just need to pay attention to a few details.

Bare root shrubs should be planted within a few days of arrival. Remove the packaging and soak roots in lukewarm water for 30 minutes to an hour. Dig a hole the same depth as the length of the roots (not any deeper) and about twice as wide as the roots' length. Build a mound of soil (taken from excavated soil) in the center of the hole with the top of the mound at ground level. Then set the shrub on top of the mound, spreading the moistened roots over it. Make sure the shrub's crown (where the roots meet the stems) is at the surface level before backfilling with soil. Hold the shrub in place with one hand and push soil into the hole with the other. Sprinkle organic rock phosphate from Espoma (follow application rate) into the hole when it is about half full. Make sure to press the soil around the roots as you go so there are no air pockets. Once the hole is filled, check once more to make sure the shrub's crown is at soil level and then tamp down with your hands. Give the shrub a good drink of water. I like to place a hose at its base and allow water to slowly trickle for 15 to 30 minutes. Make sure to water the shrub every other day for about two weeks (depending on rainfall and your soil type - e.g., sandy or clay) and then about once a week after that. Be patient! Bare roots can take several weeks before they start to push out leaves.

■ **Say no to girdling roots.** When scouting for the "best pick of the litter" at garden centers, make sure a shrub doesn't have girdling roots. This is when a root starts to coil around the base of the shrub, usually visible at the soil surface. This circling root can eventually strangle the plant. This is more common in shrubs grown as single trunk specimens, as well as with trees.

■ **How to select container or ball and burlap shrubs.** When surveying container or ball and burlap shrubs, check to make sure the shrub has been planted at the right level. As noted earlier, the crown should be at the soil surface. All too often, shrubs are planted too deeply, with inches of soil built up on the stems or trunk. This moisture, plus lack of light and air on the stems, can lead to rot and disease issues. Once again, this usually is more of a problem with single trunk shrubs.

Boy meets girl, and baby makes three (or... how hollies get their berries)

I'm referring to male and female shrubs (dioecious) that must be planted near each other for cross pollination to occur, resulting in berries. Most flowering shrubs produce both male and female flowers OR flowers with both male and female parts. But there are some, like hollies, that require matchmaking. Both evergreen and deciduous hollies need companions. And not just any companion. Most cultivars will only "mate" with specific partners (i.e., 'Blue Princess' with 'Blue Prince'). If you're not sure of your holly's sex, take a look at the small white flowers when in bloom (anytime from early spring to early summer depending on your hardiness zone and the cultivar). Female flowers only have the stigma while males only have stamens. If you discover you have a female, but are not sure of the cultivar, try pairing it with 'Blue Stallion', popular with many ladies. And this does not need to be a one-to-one relationship. One male can easily pollinate 10 or more females. Finally, if you want to take the headache out of arranged marriages, then buy shrubs in the Berri-Magic Royalty collection (or similar series) where male and female shrubs are planted together in the same pot. Masses of berries are produced, given their close proximity!

A few other commonly sold shrubs that need a male and female to produce berries are Aucuba (spotted laurel), Lindera (spicebush), Japanese skimmia (Skimmia *japonica*), Viburnum *davidii* (David Viburnum), Northern bayberry (Myrical *pensylvanica*), and Ribes (clove current).

Berri-Magic Royalty Holly

■ **A broadleaf evergreen caveat.** Fall clearance sales at garden centers attract throngs of gardeners, including me! Flowering shrubs are one of the main attractions. Fall is a fantastic time to install most woody plants. Soil temperature stays warmer longer than air temperature, plus, rainfall is usually more reliable – perfect growing conditions. Shop away! My only caveat pertains to broadleaf evergreens, like Rhododendron. After October 1, I think twice about a tempting deal (in hardiness Zones 6 or colder). It can be a risky transaction. Evergreens don't go dormant in winter; they continue to lose water (transpire) through their leaves. If a newly planted Rhododendron hasn't had enough time for its roots to get well established before the ground freezes, you can say sayonara. And that is NOT a deal.

Blue Mist Shrub (Caryopteris) 'Beyond Midnight'

Beautyberry (Callicarpa) 'Pearl Glam'

■ **If you live in snowy climes...** Spare yourself a headache and crushed plants if you live in snowy regions by planting flowering shrubs that can be pruned back to the ground in late fall or spring. Who cares how much snow piles on top of them! Great picks include Spirea (not spring flowering), blue mist shrub (Caryopteris), smooth Hydrangea (i.e. 'Annabelle'), butterfly bush, chaste tree (Vitex), bush clover (Lespedeza) and beautyberry (Callicarpa).

■ **Watch where you plant.** And speaking of crushed shrubs, be wary of using evergreens and other woody shrubs near high voltage electrical boxes or pad-mounted transformers. First, call the electrical company regarding restrictions. You can also call organizations like Dig Safe (a free service), a not-for-profit clearinghouse that notifies participating utility companies of your plans to dig. In addition to watching out for your own safety, also think carefully about the best plants to use around these boxes. Remember, utility companies must be able to access these boxes, even in winter. This can spell disaster for woody plants in the path of snow removal equipment. To minimize "plant carnage," use perennials that can be cut to the ground in fall, or annuals, in these snow removal war zones.

■ **Flower buds that aren't easily hoodwinked.** Flower buds of early blooming shrubs can be fooled into breaking dormancy with the first wave of warm weather. But if temperatures drop again, this "false start" can be costly, killing the buds. If you live in a region where early spring temperatures can be erratic, look for cultivars that are more resistant to false starts. These either bloom later or have very cold-hardy buds. Consider The Little Girl Magnolia series; Lilacs such as 'Miss Kim' (lavender-blue), 'Miss Canada' (red-pink) and 'Agnes Smith' (white); Forsythia 'Meadowlark' and 'Northern Sun'; and Azaleas in the Northern Lights series with bud hardiness up to minus 40 degrees.

Invest in shrubs that earn their keep

Flowering shrubs that embellish a landscape month after month, especially in winter, are worthy warriors. Here are a few pollinator friendly suggestions providing 12 months of interest:

Cornus *alba* 'Prairie Fire' or 'Aurea' Sun–Part Shade. Electrifying yellow leaves, white flowers, red berries, glowing red stems in winter

Ninebark (Physocarpus) Many cultivars Native; Sun–Part Sun. Great flowers, berries, many foliage colors plus exfoliating bark in winter

American Cranberrybush (Viburnum *opulus* var. *americanum*, also known as Viburnum *trilobum*) Native; Sun–Part Shade. White spring flowers, large serrated lobed leaves, bright red fruit that persists through late winter, nice fall color

Holly (evergreen and deciduous) Sun–Shade, depending on cultivar. Deciduous shrubs are native.

Fothergilla g. 'Blue Shadows' Native; Sun–Part Shade. Frosty-blue leaves, white fragrant flowers, orange-red-yellow fall foliage, silver-gray bark in winter

Oakleaf Hydrangea (Hydrangea *quercifolia*) Native; Sun–Part Shade. Long airy white flowers (some cultivars turn pretty pink in fall), burgundy-red fall foliage, peeling bark for winter interest. 'Little Honey' has gold leaves

Red Chokeberry (Aronia *arbutifolia*) Native; Sun–Part Shade. White or soft pink flowers, red fruit in summer that lasts through much of winter, brilliant red fall foliage

Ninebark (Physocarpus) 'Ginger Wine'

Tatarian Dogwood (Cornus *albus*) 'Sunshine'

Red Chokeberry (Aronia *arbutifolia*)

Bottlebrush (Fothergilla) 'Blue Shadows'

Oakleaf Hydrangea (Hydrangea *quercifolia*) 'Little Honey'

Holy Hydrangea!

Hydrangeas are the most googled flowering shrub on the internet. They generate a lot of interest, as well as confusion. Enough already. Allow me to provide some straight-shooting input and advice so you can save yourself financial and emotional stress.

There are five commonly sold species of Hydrangea. All have blooms with both sterile flowers (large showy petals to attract pollinators, yet having no pollen or nectar) and fertile flowers (much smaller, but filled with pollen and nectar). If your goal to is provide the most beneficial food source to pollinators, then choose blooms with more fertile flowers.

Smooth Hydrangea (Hydrangea *arborescens*)
'Invincibelle Ruby'

Smooth Hydrangea (Hydrangea *arborescens*)

Native. White or pink lace-cap or mophead flowers. Flowers are not prized for fall color. Flower buds form in spring on new wood so flowering is not impacted by bitter cold winters. Prune in late fall or late winter. Drought tolerant. White flowering shrubs like 'Annabelle' and 'Haas Halo' are very shade tolerant. Many cultivars hardy to Zone 3.

Smooth Hydrangea (Hydrangea *arborescens*)
Invincibelle 'Wee White'

Bigleaf Hydrangea (Hydrangea *macrophylla*)
White, pink, blue or purple lace-cap or mophead flowers. Flower color is affected by soil pH. Flowers appear in early summer and can repeat into fall depending on the cultivar. All form flower buds on old wood (in late summer or fall before the following season). Those that also bloom on new wood will set additional buds in spring. IF pruning is needed, do so in late summer. Given the frustration and confusion over pruning this group of Hydrangeas, the best practice is to buy a variety that matures to the height you want and don't prune at all! Bigleaf Hydrangeas require a lot of water. Most are hardy in Zones 5 and 6 or above. A few are hardy to Zone 4.

Mountain Hydrangea (Hydrangea *serrata*) Pink, blue or purple lace-cap or mophead flowers. These are similar to bigleaf Hydrangeas in that soil pH can affect flower color. They also can produce flower buds on old and new wood. Mountain Hydrangeas tend to have smaller leaves, losing less water from transpiration, therefore requiring less supplemental watering. Mountain Hydrangea is also prized for hardier flower buds (*serrata* is native to the mountains in Japan, while *macrophylla* is native to Japan's shoreline). Most are hardy in Zones 5 or above. A few are hardy to Zone 4.

Mophead Hydrangea (Hydrangea *macrophylla*)
Cityline 'Rio'

Mountain Hydrangea (Hydrangea *serrata*)
'Tuff Stuff Red'

Oakleaf Hydrangea (Hydrangea *quercifolia*)

Native. Long, airy white flowers. A few cultivars age to a lovey rosy-pink. Available in single or double petaled flowers ('Snowflake' is a double). Flower buds form in early fall. If pruning is needed, do so in late summer. This Hydrangea gets its common name from leaves that resemble oak leaves. The foliage turns a gorgeous burgundy-red in fall. Exfoliating bark adds winter interest. Drought tolerant. Many Oakleaf Hydrangeas can get large and equally wide (8 to 10 feet). Recent breeding has introduced compact cultivars like 'Ruby Slippers', 'Pee Wee', 'Munchkin' and 'Sikes Dwarf', all 5 feet or shorter. Hardy in Zones 5 and above.

Panicle Hydrangea (Hydrangea *paniculata*) 'Fire Light'

Panicle Hydrangea (Hydrangea *paniculata*)

White ball or pyramidal-shaped flowers. Many cultivars turn shades of pink in summer or fall. Soil pH does not affect flower color. Flower buds form in spring on new wood. Prune in late winter. Drought tolerant. Both shrub and single trunk (tree) choices are available in this group. Mature heights vary greatly, from 30 inches to over 20 feet! In addition to flower shapes, blooms can be very dense (mostly sterile flowers) or light and airy (more fertile flowers). Many hardy to Zone 3.

Oakleaf Hydrangea (Hydrangea *quercifolia*) 'Gatsby Pink'

■ **Discover Cary Award Champions.**
Winners of this prestigious horticulture award are selected for their superior performance in New England. But these outstanding plants also excel in other regions of the country. To receive this award, plants must be pest and disease resistant, hardy to at least Zone 5, easily available in the nursery trade, and provide extended, or multiple seasons of interest. Only two plants win this coveted crown each year. One of the 2017 awardees is Korean Abelia (Abelia *monsanensis*), a highly fragrant, spring-flowering shrub that is shade and drought tolerant. In addition to lovely fall foliage it is also deer resistant. Most Abelias are only hardy to Zone 7; Korean Abelia overwinters in Zone 4. For a list of exceptional shrubs, trees, vines and groundcovers visit caryaward.com.

■ **Spare the water!** Water is a precious resource, so valued that it is now being traded on the Stock Exchange. What a great segue to flowering shrubs that are highly drought tolerant. Sun-to-part-sun selections include Spirea, blue mist shrub (Caryopteris), panicle Hydrangea (Hydrangea *paniculata*), three leaf sumac (Rhus *trilobata*), butterfly bush (Buddleia), Yellow Bird of Paradise (Caesalpinia *gilliesii*), flowering quince (Chaenomeles),

Abelia 'Sunny Anniversary'

Coralberry (Symphoricarpus), sea rose (Rosa *rugosa*), Deutzia, Adam's needle (Yucca *filamentosa*) and lilac (Syringa). Some part-shade-to-shade shrubs are variegated Aralia (Eleutherococcus *sieboldianus* 'Variegatus'), Kerria *japonica*, bottlebrush buckeye (Aesculus *parviflora*), leatherleaf Mahonia (Mahonia *bealei*, listed as a Gold Medal shrub by the Pennsylvania Horticultural Society), Carolina Allspice 'Michael Lindsay' (Calycanthus *floridus*, listed as a Gold Medal shrub by the Pennsylvania Horticultural Society), Skimmia and spotted laurel (Aucuba *japonica*).

Yellow Bird of Paradise (Caesalpinia *gilliesii*)

Sweetshrub (Calycanthus) 'Michael Lindsay'

Coral Berry (Symphoricarpos) 'Proud Berry'

■ **Faster than a speeding bullet.** Sometimes you need flowering shrubs that act as if they were on steroids. Situations that might call for this robust growth could be a desperately needed privacy screen or a landscape that quickly matures for resale purposes. But this swift growth also means shrubs will need more frequent restraining (pruning). Be careful what you ask for. If you are looking for sprinters, check out Weigela (i.e. 'Wine and Roses' and 'Red Prince'), Tri-Color Willow 'Hakuro-Nishiki' (Salix *integra*), privet (Ligustrum), Rose of Sharon (Hibiscus *syriacus*, be sure to select sterile cultivars that will not seed aggressivley), Forsythia, mock orange (Philadelphus), beautyberry (Callicarpa) and Ninebark 'Diablo' (Physocarpus).

This Japanese Variegated Willow (Salix *integra*) 'Hakuro-Nishiki' was easily over 10 feet tall in this Massachusetts landscape.

Costly Rhododendron mistakes are sadly too common

Most folks assume Rhododendrons are shade plants. They are half right. The large-leaf varieties do indeed appreciate at least a half day of shade, if not full shade in warmer climates. Not so their small-leaf counterparts. These enjoy full sun to part sun. If you plant a small-leaf Rhododendron in full shade, it will soon be a no-leaf Rhododendron. How can you tell the difference? You're joking right? Large-leaf Rhododendrons have big, long ovate-shaped leaves. Small-leaf Rhododendrons have much smaller leaves, sometimes even round in appearance. Small-leaf Rhododendrons bloom earlier and don't get as tall as most large-leafs.

Large-leaf varieties should be sheltered from winter winds that quickly suck moisture from leaves. This can be very stressful, even deadly, if the ground is frozen and the plant can't recover water through its roots. To reduce stress, spray leaves in early winter

Rhododendron 'Capistrano'
(large-leaf Rhododendron)

with an anti-dessicant like Wilt-Pruf. Both large- and small-leaf Rhododendron have shallow roots that can dry out quickly. These shrubs benefit from a deep watering (if there is little natural rainfall) in fall before the ground freezes. Also apply a 2- to 3-inch layer of mulch around their base to reduce water evaporation from the soil and to keep roots cooler in summer heat. Both groups of Rhododendrons are acid-living shrubs, enjoying a soil pH in the 5.0s. If you need to lower soil pH, use elemental sulfur or Holly-tone. Finally, small-leaf Rhododendron self-clean (shed) their spent blooms after flowering. Large-leaf withered flowers should be pinched, or snapped off, just below the flower cluster for a cleaner look the rest of the growing season. If you do not do this, new buds will still form, but flowering may be reduced the following year.

Rhododendron 'Amy Cotta'
(small-leaf Rhododendron)

Home Run Red Rose

'Carefree Beauty' Rose

■ **Roses have a bad rep.** Too many people conclude that roses are a nightmare to grow and are only worth buying on Valentine's Day. Truth be told, there are some roses you would never see in my no-fuss landscape. But there are also roses that are as easy-going as Hosta. Smart selection and siting are key. First, roses love full sun and heat. Are some tolerant of less sun? Yes, but tolerant is the pivotal word. As far as selection, I mostly stick to modern shrub roses that receive high marks for beauty as well as limited need of fertilizers, pesticides and water. One such group is Earth-Kind roses. The Texas AgriLife Extension Service at Texas A&M were the first to conduct Earth-Kind rose trials, but now 27 states supervise these trials. Some prestigious, sustainable roses with Earth-Kind

laurels include 'Carefree Beauty', 'Sea Foam' and Knockout rose. To learn more about Earth-Kind Roses visit www.aggie-horticulture.tamu.edu/earthkindroses. Other praiseworthy series include Canadian Explorer, Oso Easy, Griffith Buck and Home Run.

* * *

Congratulations! You've made it through the longest chapter in the book. It was important to me to share these valuable tips from my own experiences with plants, both as a home gardener and as a professional in the garden center world. It is my hope that you, as a newly empowered plant geek, now feel better prepared to track down some fabulous plants at bargain basement prices. Chapter Two awaits. ■

PLANT SOURCES AND TREASURE MAPS

*N*ow that you are schooled in the art of scouting the finest, best priced, environmentally-friendly plants for gorgeous landscapes, it is time to hit the ground running. The next course in The Academy of Shrewd Plant Hunters focuses on tracking down the best sources for acquiring these gems.

I'm going to suggest a range of venues that serve up plant treasures – some may surprise you. Most people automatically think of garden centers and mail order. Not bad. But I'm also going to share some more unusual suggestions, and I'm not talking about dumpster diving. Let's start with the two most conventional sources.

GARDEN CENTERS AND NURSERIES

Weston Nurseries, in Hopkinton and Chelmsford, MA, is a full scale garden center with helpful displays and services to assist patrons with all of their gardening needs.

I am a huge advocate of shopping local and supporting family-owned garden businesses. Having worked for years with many owners at garden centers, I know how demanding and unpredictable this trade can be. These families have a love of horticulture and sharing this passion with others. It certainly isn't just for the money.

Shopping at your local garden center has many advantages over mail order:

■ **Hands-on shopping.** You see the inventory. You can pick up and "squeeze the melon," so to speak, to evaluate which is the best. For some, this hands-on investigation is part of the thrill of the hunt!

■ **Less stress on the plants.** They don't undergo the shipping stress that can occur with mail order deliveries. Stress can impact how quickly a plant adjusts to its new home.

■ **No guesswork.** When you buy a plant at a garden center you don't have to guess about its arrival condition. The plant should look the same way it did when you bought it (unless you left it in a hot car for hours with the windows closed). Plus, there is no question that the plant is in good condition (you picked it out!), whereas the appearance of some mail order plants can look questionable (especially bare root).

You control when plants arrive at your home because you're in charge of the "delivery," not the person shipping them to you.

■ **You're better informed.** You shouldn't have to wonder if a plant will successfully overwinter in your garden. Most nurseries sell landscape plants that are cold-hardy for their area.

■ **Seeing is believing.** You can clearly see a flower's true color and blooming habit, whereas some catalogs have overly intense, unnatural-looking, Photoshopped images.

■ **Size can matter.** Plants at garden centers are typically much larger and more mature than what you can get through mail order.

■ **Personalized service.** Customer service is a high priority at garden centers. You can get answers face-to-face from knowledgeable staff, who offer input about a plant's hardiness zone and cultural needs as well as give helpful tips. Mail order catalogs are a poor substitute for this level of assistance,and some catalogs dramatically stretch the truth! Many garden centers also offer plant diagnostic centers to help answer questions and suggest

Merrifield Garden Center in Fairfax, VA

solutions for critter damage, insect and disease issues, and soil health including soil pH tests. An exceptional garden center isn't just about plants; it's also about full service and relationships.

■ **Design ideas.** Many garden centers maintain lovely display beds that show mature plants and suggested combinations.

■ **Expanded seasonal inventory.** Most garden centers have fresh inventory arriving

This is one of the beautiful display beds at Prairie Moon Nursery in Winona, MN.

throughout the growing season, so there is no pressure to buy everything in spring. This is in contrast to mail order companies where popular plants can sell out early. Don't hesitate to ask garden center staff to search their vendors for a special plant if you don't see it in the inventory. Or perhaps instead of larger pots, you need small plant plugs, sold in trays, for expansive planting areas. You will never know if this is a possibility unless you ask!

■ **Easy recycling.** Many garden centers now have recycling bins for plastic pots. This is a nice convenience and eco-friendly.

6 Tips for getting the most out of your shopping experience at garden centers

1. **Sign up** for gardening newsletters and customer rewards programs. Benefits include early notices about sales and events as well as weekly specials. Rewards programs will vary, but all extend some financial incentive for shopping at their business.

2. **Know when to go.** If you are looking for a number of plant recommendations, garden design ideas, or simply have many questions, don't expect lots of personal attention and time on a weekend, especially in spring! This is peak rush hour. Rather, pick a day during the week, or go early on a weekend morning, or when it's raining. Now you have their dedicated attention!

3. **Watch for plant sales** that save you bundles of money, especially in fall when garden centers are emptying their benches and greenhouses. A few of my favorites: $35 for as many containers as you can jam into a cart, and all you can carry for $10! I wish I had videoed these creative antics. In addition to outrageous fall sales, some garden centers also pull out all stops in July, to clear out older inventory and make room for fresh material. One premier garden center in Vermont promotes a "Cartload Sale" in July. Fill a cart with as many greenhouse annuals and vegetables as possible for only $40; plus, newsletter subscribers receive a $5 coupon for additional savings.

4. **Ask!** Don't be shy about asking for a discount on less than ideal looking plants. But don't ask for free plants! This rubs most staff the wrong way. Garden centers are a business, not a charity. Instead, ask if they would consider a percentage off the price or perhaps sell two for the price of one.

Claussen's Florist, Greenhouses & Perennial Farm in Colchester, VT runs a spectacular "Cartload Sale" every July that draws customers from far and wide!

5. **"Rescue me!"** With the new emphasis on greener living and protecting the environment, you can become a "Plant Rescuer." This certainly sounds more dignified than "dumpster diver." You might politely ask a manager if you could "save" plants that were going to be thrown away because they were not up to the garden center's standard. The time and staff effort required to nurse these plants back to retail-ready shape doesn't make financial sense. You could offer a flat fee to save these plants – or a tray of fresh baked cookies! Even better would be to use some or all of these rescued plants for a restoration or community beautification project or some other good-will mission.

6. **Get to know a staff member.** Developing a loyal relationship can result in unexpected dividends, such as when employees have the opportunity to take home free plants that were removed from inventory or dozens of bags of free bulbs placed in the staff room because floor space had to be cleared for Christmas displays.

Many consumers love shopping the internet. Talk about convenience and accessibility! The U.S. Census Bureau reported that in 2016 e-commerce sales totaled $394.9 billion and were up 15.1% over 2015.

For those in the plant world, this trend can be good, or bad, depending on which side of the plant rack you're on. Most family-owned garden centers have felt a negative impact from online competition.

Online shopping has opened up the plant world to gardeners' fingertips. It is easier than ever to purchase unusual or rare plants. Even Amazon is getting into the plant sale market!

The Garden Watchdog: a useful resource

Before sharing tips on how to make the most of online orders, I need to introduce you to an amazing resource, **The Garden Watchdog**, hosted on Dave's Garden, a website for gardeners around the world (davesgarden.com/products/gwd/). The Garden Watchdog is a free directory of 7,868 mail order gardening companies that includes gardeners' opinions about a company's plant quality, price and customer service. This is a must-visit site if you have never ordered from a company. The site also allows you to search by plant to find vendors that sell it, as well as a section dedicated to finding businesses and attractions in your local region (including Christmas tree farms, farm stands, public and private gardens). My favorite feature is The Watchdog 30, which lists the top 30 most highly rated companies within their entire database. For example, New Hampshire Hostas, located near me, has made the top 30 list for the past five years.

Lazy S'S Farm and Nursery (a Garden Watchdog Top 30 company) has an inventory of over 2000+ varieties of perennials, shrubs and trees, including many rare and unusual specimens.

Broken Arrow Nursery in Hamden, CT, offers exceptional rare and unusual plants, both at their retail store and online.

Now, on to some of the *advantages* to shopping online:

■ **Time and labor-saving convenience.** You can do all your shopping from home and have the plants delivered to your doorstep.
■ **Greater selection!** Many catalogs offer a much greater selection than can possibly be offered at local nurseries – especially when it comes to recently introduced or hard-to-find varieties.
■ **Plant Replacement and Guarantee Policies.** Replacement policies vary greatly by company. Breck's offers a lifetime guarantee – for as long

as YOU garden. Despite this generous offer, they get mixed reviews from customers on The Garden Watchdog. Some companies guarantee plants for a year, others for the current growing season and some simply state that plants must arrive in good shape. READ THE FINE PRINT! Still, guarantee policies are usually better than what you can find at local nurseries.
■ **Collections of pre-planned gardens or mini-groupings.** Some catalogs offer complete garden plans and the plants at bargain prices, which can save you a lot of money if you had to pay for the plants separately, as well as the design service.

Starter Garden
5' x 12' (24 varieties, 24 plants)
Designed with learning in mind. This sampler of easy care perennials offers a full season of interest. The different foliage heights, textures and colorful flowers will highlight why perennials are prized in flower borders everywhere. The perfect gift to introduce someone special to the joys of gardening. All of our gardens include detailed instructions to ensure success. For full sun.
STARTG $219.95

Bluestone Perennials has many attractive, pre-planned design and plant packages.

Prairie Moon Nursery specializes in native plants, offering bare root, potted and assorted seeds for sale.

■ **Incredible access to native plants.** The increasing demand for native plants has generated a surge in mail order companies dedicated to natives. Some companies with good ratings on The Garden Watchdog: A Nearly Native Nursery, Prairie Moon Nursery, Mail-Order Natives, Niche Gardens, and High Country Gardens. Also, gardenlist.com/Natives.html has a large list of mail order companies that deal primarily in North American natives.

Interest in natives has also spawned educational online resources that provide lists of regionally appropriate natives. Gardeners can easily access these lists, make notes of ones they're interested in, and then shop for these at local garden centers or online. A few trustworthy sites are:

- **The National Wildlife Federation:** nwf.org/NativePlantFinder
- **Doug Tallamy's research:** BringingNatureHome.net/what-to-plant.html
- **Lady Bird Johnson Wildflower Center:** wildflower.org/plants-main (includes a resource to find businesses that sell native plants or seeds)

■ **Bargain Prices.** Careful. Not all bargain or slashed prices are really a bargain. But some truly are. To get their true value, you need to take into account the pot size (these can range from 3-inch pots to gallon-size or larger) plus shipping and handling costs. More often than not, better prices are offered when multiples of the same plants are purchased. But use your common sense. If a deal sounds too good to be true, you're probably right! One website I visited listed Bargain Bags as a shopping category. You can get 10 assorted summer blooming Lilium bulbs for only $9.99. What it doesn't say is the size or age of the bulbs and what cultivars are actually in the mix.

I was shocked to see these tiny (2-inch wide by 3-inch deep), stressed perennials after paying $54.91 online.

■ **Save on sales tax.** Usually. Read the order form.

9 Tips for Placing Orders with Mail Order Companies

1. Remain calm and think clearly. Don't become stupefied by dazzling catalogs and insane offers. It's interesting that many mail order companies with mixed reviews on The Garden Watchdog are also companies with flashy incentives to place your order. Don't let the razzle-dazzle fool you.

2. Be wary of catalogs that portray flowers with sensational, hard-to-believe colors or monstrous blooms. Trust your gut. Then look into the company's rating on The Garden Watchdog.

3. Be alert to exaggeration and sneaky terminology. On a similar note, some catalog companies have remarkably talented wordsmiths who write plant descriptions. They can make a pile of poo seem like a gold mine. The more flowery adjectives I read, the more suspicious I get. I feel the same way about exclamation marks! And some are just off the map when it comes to listing hardiness zones. This irresponsible and confusing reporting can lead many gardeners, especially newbies, down the compost path.

Here are examples of zonal double-talk:

'Orange Turmoil' Dahlia. Iridescent beauty! With an almost indescribable colour palette, our dazzling 'Orange Turmoil' Dahlia makes its presence known with full, fluffy flowers in a kaleidoscope of hues. Zones: 3–10, lift in Zones 3–7.

Another catalog of similar repute provides two recommended zone listings for each plant. For example: *Double tuberous Begonias, Suitable Zones: 3–10. Hardy Zones: 9–10.*

4. A downside: small pots. As mentioned earlier, most mail order plants come in small pots. Small pots mean small roots. Plants with smaller roots require more pampering than larger, more established root systems. Less mature plants require frequent watering and may need protection from harsh weather while getting established. Plants will also take longer to go into flower, maybe not until the second year, or even later. The financial savings

Mixed double tuberous Begonias

On the left is a container of perennial plumbago at a garden center for $17.99. On the right is a mail order pot that contained a "sprig" of plumbago for which I paid $11.98 (including shipping).

6. Good deals. Usually there are discount or freebie incentives for volume orders or orders by a specified date. This can also include free shipping. Combining an order with friends increases the total sale and may qualify for some great deals.

7. Guarantees. Take advantage of one-year guarantee policies. If you really want a plant that is borderline hardy in your area, then order it from a company that offers a minimum one-year guarantee. Now you can trial it risk free.

8. Don't get more than you asked for. Some mail order companies sell your contact information to other companies. Thankfully, due to spam regulations, they cannot do this without your permission. You need to find the teeny-weeny box buried in the order form and then check NO to stop them from selling your name. Use a magnifying glass. One company requires that you WRITE a letter and mail it to a P.O. box to request that your name not be shared.

Coral Bark Maple (Acer *palmatum*) 'Sango-Kaku'

associated with mail order are usually swapped for additional time, effort and patience on your part. I hate to sound too harsh, but time is money. You decide what you have more of.

5. About delivery dates. Check to see if delivery dates are listed for your hardiness zone. If not, ask! Or better yet, specify a date (week) that you wish to receive the shipment so you are ready when the little (or big) brown box lands on your porch.

The arrival state of perennial plumbago (Ceratostigma *plumbaginoides*). I purchased this "specimen" for $8.99 plus shipping from a mail order company to remain unnamed...

9. Before you commit... Make sure to check the customer satisfaction statement concerning a plant's arrival state, as well as the return policy. If these are not clearly stated, strike number one. Call and find out! If the phone number is not easily found, strike two. And if you don't want a substitute plant for one that is sold out, note it on the form, and indicate if you want a refund or credit towards a future order. If this isn't an option, strike three – toss the catalog into the recycling bin.

Let's explore additional "plant dispenser" sources, as well as some unusual hiding places for great plant finds.

Big Box Stores and Supermarkets

As a loyal customer of family-owned garden businesses, a shudder goes up my spine as I write this. But the reality is that many premier plant companies, like Proven Winners, Monrovia and First Editions, are shipping material to these venues. And usually the prices are substantially less, as is the amount of attention the plants receive.

If you are going to buy plants at places like Home Depot, Lowes and Wal-Mart, purchase them as soon as they roll off the delivery trucks while the plants are still fresh, well watered and tended. After this, plants can descend into "plant hell." Instead of guessing when a truck will arrive,

check with staff. Per Ann Whitman, author of *Organic Gardening for Dummies* (Hungry Minds, 2001), "There's a schedule in every store that notes when the trucks will arrive and what they are carrying. Ask an employee to check for you." She also recommends making a deal at the end of the season, before Christmas trees and other holiday décor arrive. She states that she has heard of customers buying everything left on the lot for $100.

When shopping for plants at these sources, however, do not expect knowledgeable advice and service from the sales staff. You get what you pay for.

Many leading plant companies now sell their product at big box stores

I rarely salute big box stores but here's a high five to Home Depot. This megastore now requires all plants that have been treated with neonicotinoids (systemic pesticides that kill many bugs, including beneficial ones) to bear a special tag informing customers that the plant has been exposed to this insecticide.

This plant is protected from problematic

APHIDS
WHITE FLIES
BEETLES
MEALY BUGS
and other unwanted pests by Neonicotinoids

Online Ordering and Free Shipping Service to Your Local Garden Center

Brilliant! Monrovia, one of the largest plant wholesalers in the country, offers a wide variety of plants for direct sale to the public. You place an order online at shop.monrovia.com and the plants are shipped for FREE to a participating garden center near you. The garden center notifies you when your order has arrived for pick-up. For a charge, you can have the plants delivered to your home (as well as installed).

Red Oak seedlings at the New York State Department of Conservation's tree farm.

Your County Soil & Water Conservation Department; County Conservation Department

If you have time and patience, these plants are ludicrously cheap. Plants are sold bare root or as seedlings. Inventory can include trees, shrubs, conifers and groundcovers. Native plants are usually featured. As an example of pricing, the New York State Department of Conservation has a tree farm in Saratoga Springs (near where I used to live). You could buy 25 two-year-old hardwood trees like Red Oak and American Hazelnut for $30. Or 25 three-year-old Balsam Fir for $20.

Farmers Markets

There are many feel-good reasons for shopping at farmers markets. In addition to a wealth of fresh, seasonable food, you are also supporting local farmers and connecting with the community. Plus you can find home-grown nursery plants for excellent prices! The United States Department of Agriculture maintains a directory of farmers markets that includes location, operating times, vendors, products, and much more. It's a fabulous resource. Check it out at www.ams.usda.gov/local-food-directories/farmersmarkets

Botanical Gardens, Arboretums, Plant and Horticultural Societies

Membership in these not-for-profit organizations supports horticulture, science, research and educational programs for a broad audience, and you receive amazing benefits including access to uncommon plants. For example, my membership in the Massachusetts Horticultural Society came with a $25 gift certificate to a top-end garden center as well as a ticket to the Boston Flower and Garden Show. Plant sales, raffles and swaps are also some of the bonuses. It is not uncommon for members to have first dibs on plants for sale. I attended one plant society meeting where members

divided plants from their gardens and had them for sale at bargain prices. After the meeting ended, any plants remaining were snagged by those that stayed behind to clean up. I helped clean up.

Berkshire Botanical Garden's annual spring plant sale always has striking and unusual plants.

Flower and Garden Shows

Okay, I admit it. I'm a plant vulture at these events. I soar around landscape displays noting "prey" I hope to snatch at the end of the show. Many landscape companies and nurseries are happy to unload plants at absurd prices instead of having to cart these back to the nursery. If a plant (or decorative piece) interests you, ask if it will be for sale when the show closes. If the answer is yes, then join other savvy gardeners who show up at the closing hours.

I took this photo of a floor display at a green industry trade show.

Green Industry Trade Shows and Expos

Plant vendors at green industry trade shows can experience the same fatigue at the end of an event as display merchants at flower shows. Great deals await those who are in the right place at the right time (and sometimes there's actually a "free for the taking" area tucked away at the back of the show space). The tricky part is getting into a trade show since most are not open to the general public, only to those in the industry (owners and employees). This is where friends in "green" places can help. Ask if there is a way for you to attend the show under their company name or membership. Badges are required for show access. Perhaps they can help you. You'll never know unless you ask!

Landscape Crews

Be on the lookout for garden or landscape projects that involve plant removal, including spring blooming bulbs. It is not uncommon that these dislocated plants are heading to a big compost pile, and many green waste disposal sites charge landscapers a dumping fee. Grab your "Plant Rescuer" cape and pleasantly ask if the plants are being thrown out, and if so, would it be okay to recycle some into your garden. Not only are you saving the landscapers a dumping fee, you are also saving yourself money and giving displaced plants a second chance. Agreed, this requires chutzpah, but where there is a will, there is chutzpah.

Other People's Homes

Homes for sale with lovely gardens. Having sold a home with lots of gardens, I knew there were only so many divisions of my cherished plants that I could take with me. The rest (especially perennials) were at the mercy of the next owner. Sadly, most new homeowners will not have the same love affair with the gardens as their former caretaker – you. Many gardens will fall into disarray; others totally removed. How much better if some plants could be sold (or given) to another dedicated gardener before the deed transfer!

Homes NOT for sale with lovely gardens. Who doesn't enjoy hearing words of praise for hard work well done? More specifically, heartfelt accolades for a beautiful flower garden? I can't count the times I have walked up to an unknown gardener in their yard and gushed about how gorgeous the gardens were. And the same in reverse has happened to me in my own gardens. Of course these compliments have no ulterior motive! When you see gifted artwork, it's hard not to give verbal applause. But sometimes you may be surprised with a little gift in return – some seeds, a division, an extra seedling. Many gardeners have generous, passionate spirits and enjoy sharing plants with others, just as others have done for them.

Homes not long for this world. Demolition crews are fun to stalk. If you notice a home or business being torn down with salvageable plants around it, "chutzpah" over and see if they will let you rescue them before the bulldozer arrives.

Students in the Department of Urban Horticulture & Design at SUNY Farmingdale State College grow almost all of the plants sold at this huge annual Plant Sale.

Spring Fundraisers

Arbor Day and Earth Day fundraisers can be gold mines for low-priced flowering plants. Plus, many garden clubs host gigantic plant sales in May and June as their primary funding source. Be a good samaritan and help them out! Master Gardeners also host great sales. Just keep in mind, if you see lots of one particular plant for sale, it is probably a sign that it can spread quickly. Think twice before you grab a pot.

School Horticulture Projects

Put on your Inspector Clouseau hat and check out what happens to plants at high schools and colleges with horticulture programs. Greenhouses filled with plants grown during semester projects need to be emptied before the next class starts. Our local BOCES vocational school held phenomenal sales.

SUNY Farmingdale State College has a HUGE sale each spring. Almost all of the plants are grown by students. The income supports student intern programs, facility upgrades and supplements the Department of Urban Horticulture & Design's budget.

Plant Trial Winners

Don't take off your sleuthing hat yet. Scope out what happens to "guinea pig plants" in plant trial evaluation programs. Many of these evaluations are conducted at botanical gardens, arboretums and universities. The top performers in these comparative trials are then recommended to gardeners as well as to the horticulture industry. Once a trial is finished, some "blue ribbon" plants are relocated to the trial organization's display

The Ledyard Garden Club of CT hosts a gigantic plant sale every spring. Proceeds go to the club's community and civic projects and charitable donations.

beds. Poor performers and thugs usually end up in the compost pile. The remaining plants are given away to staff, volunteers and others. If you can't volunteer, then try to be an "other."

Seed and Plant Swaps

There is quite an extensive online community interested in exchanging plants and ideas. One such group is called The GardenWeb Forum. The site has many sections including Exchanges and Trading (http://forums.gardenweb.com/forums/exchind and http://forums2.gardenweb.com/forums/the-seed-exchange). You can sort by state, region and plant category (i.e., Daylily, Hosta, Allium). Other sources for seed and plant exchanges are your local garden clubs and horticultural groups.

There are lots of goodies to check out at the annual Spring Green Thumb Perennial Swap in Warrensburg, NY.

Host Your Own Swap

Move aside, Pampered Chef and Stella & Dot jewelry parties. It's time to host a plant swap shindig! All gardeners (like me) with dirt under their cracked nails are invited, as well as folks with more common sense. Everyone must bring at least one plant divided from their garden (or purchased at a local garden center). You leave with the same number of plants that you brought (ideally, plants should be different than the ones you brought, unless you stopped at a garden center). Add to the festivities by serving garden-themed drinks like Summer Peach Old-Fashioned and Watermelon-Mint Mojitos (for more creative ideas, read my friend Amy Stewart's book, *The Drunken Botanist*). Toss in some nasturtium blossom appetizers, turn up the music, and start dancing in your muck boots!

Seed libraries are "growing" all over the country. This seed lending library is at Richmond Public Library in Richmond, CA.

Seed Libraries

Public libraries are now part of the movement to prevent further loss of genetic diversity in the plant world and to encourage more people to start gardening. Library members "check out" seed for free, grow the plants, harvest seeds, and "return" some of these to replenish the library's seed inventory. To see if there is a seed library near you or to learn how to start one, visit these sites: Seed Library Social Network (seedlibraries.org) and Global Map of Seed Libraries (seedlibrarymap.com).

Turn around!

You might have a propagator's jackpot in your own yard! Take a fresh look at your plants and see which ones can be divided. Or perhaps there are seeds to harvest or bulblets to collect? Why not take stem or root cuttings? The only cost to you is a little effort. My first book, *The Ultimate Flower Gardener's Top Ten Lists*, has a whole section devoted to dividing perennials. Another fabulous resource that provides a wealth of how-to propagating steps (including grafting, layering, collecting fern spores) is Penn State Extension's Master Gardener Manual. This 800-page book covers gardening from A to Z and is available for anyone to purchase. Simply go to extension.psu.edu/publications/agrs-139/view. In addition to these books, there are many others on the market, including one by my friend Ken Druse, titled *Making More Plants: The Science, Art, and Joy of Propagation*.

I listed this shrub and perennial collection (Azaleas, Hydrangea, Elderberry 'Lemony Lace', purple Bee Balm) on Craig's list for $45. It sold quickly!

Craig's List

Surprised? I've sold a number of my perennials and flowering shrubs on Craig's List. Go to Farm & Garden and type in plants (or perennials, shrubs, etc.) While you are on Craig's List, check the free section for plants, gardening tools and products.

Freecycle.org

This is an interesting organization. The home page states, "It's a grassroots and entirely nonprofit movement of people who are giving (and getting) stuff for free in their own towns and neighborhoods. It's all about reuse and keeping good stuff out of landfills." You type in your city and state and up pops a resource page listing All Items, Offers and Wanted. You can fine-tune your search by typing in what you are looking for – plants.

This stunning crape myrtle was listed on Craig's List for $5 (24-inch tall plants) by a wholesale grower who wanted to unload surplus inventory.

Plant Babysitting Programs

Some plant groups, such as the Daylily Society *(Hemerocallis)*, have babysitting plant programs. Only members with good standings can be babysitters. Costlier new daylily cultivars are purchased directly from breeders by the club. A "babysitter" is then given a plant for free to grow in their garden until it becomes a large clump that can be divided into multiple fans. The daylily is dug up and fans are auctioned off to club members. The babysitter gets to keep two fans at no charge for their nanny services. A few Hosta and Iris societies have similar programs.

Garage sales

Russian roulette. You could walk away with a priceless treasure or your worst nightmare. If you are plant savvy, the odds are you'll have sweet dreams. I used to sell divisions from my gardens during our annual village garage sale. I know people were thrilled with

This unusual Japanese Painted Fern, 'Burgundy Lace', was always a popular item at my division sales.

their bargain-priced purchases and I was happy to have cash for new plants! But then again, I have seen people skipping gleefully away from a garage sale holding a pot of Bishops Weed, unaware of the plant terrorist that was going home with them.

An employee perk

I loved working part time at garden centers. Not only did I learn a lot (which eventually led to starting my own business), but I also received an employee discount on purchases. Many garden centers offer this employee perk, given the pay is not lucrative and it is a seasonal position (usually spring through June). ■

DESIGN SECRETS THAT SAVE MONEY AND TIME

*N*ow that you are savvy shopper, knowing the ins and outs of selecting and sourcing the best plants for the best prices, let's take this penny-pinching theme one step further. It's time to combine and arrange the plants for an eye-catching, sustainable design that requires little input from you, as well as from water or additional nutrients.

In this chapter I outlined five colorful, time-saving design themes:

Vine-yards
Living Rugs
Xeric Gardens
(with a focus on gravel gardens)
The Right-Size Meadow Garden
A 3-Season Garden Trifecta

But don't limit yourself to only these suggestions. There is a wealth of ideas out there for beautiful, no-fuss, environmentally-beneficial designs…including those inspired by:

- Botanical gardens and arboretums
- The Garden Conservancy's Open Days program
- Public parks, flower and garden shows
- Local garden tours
- And of course, Pinterest.

'Brakelights Red Yucca' stops traffic with its red blooms.

VINE-YARDS

Up, Down and All Around

Flowering vines are usually relegated to climbing trellises or arbors, yet they are so much more versatile! We need to stop labeling them as simply climbers. Flowering vines make breathtaking displays cascading over retaining walls and tumbling down slopes. They also excel as cost-effective, weed-suppressing ground covers. A living rug of intertwining flowering vines will be the talk of the neighborhood! Living privacy walls is another one of their talents. Flowering vines are not one-trick ponies!

There are so many cost-saving advantages to vines – annual, perennial or woody. Vines typically require less water and fertilizer. And,

Sweet Autumn Clematis creates a cascading waterfall as a backdrop to a lovely public garden in Albany, NY.

Clematis 'Arabella' creates a charming ground cover next to yellow Sedge (Acorus).

depending on the mature stem length (did you notice I didn't say *height*?), one vine can fill the space that would require multiples of other plants. Routine maintenance such as pruning and deadheading is also minimal when you garden with easy-care vines like the ones featured in this design segment.

Before I go any further writing about blockbuster vines, let's review first the three ways "climbing" vines achieve their goal. This is especially relevant if your intention is to use them for vertical interest. ALL can be used as ground covers or cascaders.

Simply stated, vines fall into the following categories:

Twiners

These acrobats use tendrils (stem or leaf) or twining stems to launch themselves skyward. Tendril-type vines include Clematis, Sweet Pea and grape vines. Threadlike tendrils are only about an inch long so they need something thin and skinny to wrap around, usually no more than 1/4-inch diameter. Possible "ladders" include lattice, string, mesh, netting and chain link fence.

Vines that wrap their entire stems around a structure include Wisteria, Honeysuckle, Morning Glory and Black-Eyed Susan Vine. Stem twiners can either climb clockwise or counterclockwise.

Golden Hops and Clematis playing nicely on my obelisk.

Annual Sweet Pea (Lathyrus *odoratus*) adds beauty and intense fragrance as it weaves through a wire fence

Most climb counterclockwise, but Golden Hops (Humulus *lupulus* 'Aureus') and American Wisteria head clockwise. If a stem twiner just flops and never advances, try coiling the vine in the opposite direction. Presto! Be aware that some "goliath" twiners, like Wisteria, need a very sturdy support to wrap around.

Clingers

These vines use either aerial roots or adhesive pads to advance. Climbing Hydrangea and Euonymus are examples with aerial roots; Boston Ivy and Virginia Creeper have pads.

Rambling Red Rose sweeps up one side of my arbor to greet the outstretched branches of Tricolor European Beech tree.

Virginia Creeper 'Red Wall' (Parthenocissus *quinquefolia*) on a chain link fence

Scramblers or Ramblers

These vines cannot ascend on their own; they need a helping hand. Or just allow them to flow over walls, slopes and containers. "Climbing" roses and Bougainvillea are examples. These need twine or some type of attachment device to assist them heavenward.

I must take a moment to say a word about Clematis, given the frequency of questions I receive about it.

Clematis are grouped into three categories based on when they form flower buds and, correspondingly, when you prune them.

Group 1 (also called A): These develop flower buds on old wood – similar to Forsythia, Lilac and Rhododendron. If pruning is required, do so right after they finish flowering.

Clematis 'Rebecca' Group 2.

Clematis *montana* 'Marjorie' Group 1.

Group 2 (also called B): These bloom on old and new wood. Light pruning can be done after the first and second flowering.

Group 3 (also called C): I love this group. I call them no-brainers. Group 3 Clematis only produce flowers on new wood, which means they can be pruned almost to the ground in fall or early spring.

To learn more about the world of Clematis and their care, visit Brushwood Nursery's website (brushwoodnursery.com). The owner, Dan Long, is a highly respected "vine man," especially on Clematis.

Clematis 'Cassis' Group 3.

Clematis *virginiana* ■ Native; Sun–Part Shade; 12'–20' tall; Late Summer–Fall; Zone 3–8. Fragrant flowers. Alternative to aggressive Sweet Autumn Clematis (Clematis *terniflora* or *paniculata*).

Perennial Sweet Pea (Lathyrus *latifolius*) ■ Sun–Part Shade; 6'–8' tall; Early Summer; Zone 5–9

Climbing Rose 'William Baffin' ■ Sun–Part Shade; 10' tall; Summer; Zone 3–10

Bougainvillea ■ Sun; 6'–30' depending on the variety; Spring through Fall; Zone 9–11. Many flower colors. Thornless varieties available.

Lonicera *sempervirens* **'Major Wheeler'** ■ Native;
Sun–Part Sun; 6'–8' tall; Summer; Zone 4–9;
deer resistant

Wisteria *frutescens* **'Amethyst Falls'** ■ Native;
Sun–Part Sun; 15'–30'; Late Spring–Early Summer;
Zone 5–9

Schizophragma 'Moonlight' ■ Part Sun–Shade;
10'–15'+ tall; Summer; Zone 5–9

Purple Passion Flower (Passiflora *incarnata*) ■
Native; Sun–Part Shade; 6'–8' tall; Summer; Zone 5–9

Annuals (or Tropicals)

Corkscrew Vine (Vigna *caracalla*) ▪ Sun; 10'–20' tall; Summer; Zone 9–11. A favorite of Thomas Jefferson.

Rex Begonia Vine (Cissus *discolor*) ▪ Part Shade–Shade; 6'–10' tall; grown for its foliage; Zone 10–11

Cup and Saucer Vine (Cobaea *scandens*) ▪ Sun; up to 20' tall; Summer; Zone 9–11

Gloriosa Lily (Gloriosa *superba*) ▪ Sun–Part Shade; 4'–6' tall; Mid-Summer–Early Fall; Zone 8–10

LIVING RUGS
Plant a Handmade Area Rug

I'm not your typical quilter, weaver or seamstress. My workroom is the garden and the materials are plants. I delight in creating living rugs that are packed with color and require minimum care. These rugs are self-cleaning – no vacuuming or sweeping required. They never fade; they become thicker over time, not threadworn. These weed-smothering mats can be left out in winter. Water conservation and controlling erosion are a few more prized attributes. Plus, living rugs are easy to fabricate and they're inexpensive.

Long-lived, drought-tolerant ground covers are the foundation for these durable, highly-valued area rugs. Other accessories, such as spring-

Perennial Laurentia weaves itself around patio stones.

Creeping Sedums make a colorful, weed-suppressing mat.

blooming bulbs and no-fuss annuals, can be used like ties on a quilt. Not only are living rugs attractive, they also save you time and money. Weeding is minimal and labor-intensive, pricey mulch is a thing of the past.

Before outlining the simple steps for fashioning your work of art, I want to note that I will not be mentioning Vinca, Pachysandra or Liriope. It's a safe bet that you already know about these commonly used ground covers. These are usually used as solo plantings anyway. I'm talking about creating a kaleidoscope of color from a mixed planting that parades eye-catching foliage and pollinator-friendly flowers over three seasons, if not longer.

Assembling the materials

Ground covers are commonly sold in flats or small, 3- or 4-inch containers. Two popular series are STEPABLES and Jeepers Creepers. An online source, Classy Groundcovers (classygroundcovers.com), is a top rated mail order company offering free shipping. They sell "ground cover packages" that number 15 or more plants per package. Customers can choose from packages that contain only one type of plant or those featuring mixed selections.

Sedum Tiles: another great option. These are easy and stylish – just drop and grow! Depending on the grower, vegetated coconut coir mats (packed with mixed sedum plugs) usually range in size from 12 x 24 inches to 10 x 20 inches. "Sedum sod" rolls are also available for larger spaces. Sedum Tiles are sold at garden centers, box stores and online.

Sedum Tiles are easy to "install" and low maintenance.

Site Prep

Proper site prepping is essential for thriving "mulch rugs." These colorful, labor-saving, living carpets will be around for years! Start by removing any weeds or grass. Don't take a shortcut on this important step. If you do, you'll be playing a game of Twister as you awkwardly stretch between establishing ground cover squares to reach weeds.

After the site is weed free, spread 2 to 3 inches of organic matter (i.e., compost, manure, leaf mold) over the soil and scratch this into the top few inches. Test a sample mixture for its soil pH. If a correction is needed, apply lime or sulfur at the recommended rate before planting.

An alternative to working organic matter into the soil (which can actually bring dormant weed seeds to the surface and be a headache later), is to place layers of newspaper over the weed-free area. (Or buy rolls of recycled landscape paper.) Wet the paper and then cover with 2 to 3 inches of topsoil mixed with organic matter. You can blend the "ingredients" yourself or purchase pre-mixed product.

Planting

Now the "room" is ready to be "carpeted." Start setting out ground covers in staggered rows, geometric patterns or other creative shapes. In general, allow 8 to 12 inches between plants, although the container size (maturity of the plant) may dictate otherwise. Obviously, the closer you space plants, the faster the soil surface is covered and weeding is eliminated. Before actually digging, step back and make sure you are pleased with the rug's design. Then plant away. Before backfilling holes, sprinkle organic, slow-release, granular fertilizer, such as Plant-Tone, around roots. Water the bed well afterwards and apply a 2-inch layer of mulch (i.e., finely shredded, undyed wood) in between the plants to keep weeds out and conserve moisture.

Carpet Care

The ground covers in the following plant lists are drought tolerant...BUT they will still require extra attention for the first year or two after planting. Depending on your hardiness zone, regional weather (rain, wind, humidity), and if the location is sunny or shady, you may need to water the "carpet" once or twice a week for the first few weeks, and then once a week after that (again, natural rainfall and the other above-mentioned factors will impact how often watering is needed).

The other important bit of maintenance will be keeping weeds from "staining" the rug as it fills in.

Let 'em Run!

Now let's take a look at some sturdy, eye-pleasing ground covers to weave into your design. All of the recommended, drought tolerant perennials spread either by rhizomes (underground stems) or stems that root where leaf nodes touch the ground.

On the following pages you'll meet 12 of my favorites.

Along with a plant's general information (i.e., light requirement, hardiness zone range), I note also its tolerance for foot traffic: none (N), low (L), moderate (MO) or high (H); and speed of "travel": slow (S), medium (M) or fast (F). Keep in mind that plants listed for Sun to Part Sun will appreciate more shade in warmer zones (7 or higher). And given that we are talking about "enthusiastic" plants, some may be invasive in parts of the country. Please check with your regional extension office or garden center for a plant's appropriateness in your area.

Ground Covers for Sun to Part Sun

FOOT TRAFFIC TOLERANCE:	SPEED OF TRAVEL:
none (N) low (L) moderate (MO) high (H)	slow (S) medium (M) fast (F)

Ice Plant (Delosperma *cooperi*) ■ 3"–6" tall; Summer; Zone 5–11; N, M

Red Creeping Thyme (Thymus *praecox* 'Coccineus') ■ 2"–4" tall; Summer; Zone 3–8; MO–H, M

Pink Knotweed Magic Carpet (Persicaria *capitata*) 'Magic Carpet' ■ 3"–6" tall; Summer; Zone 7–10; L, M–F

Russian Stonecrop (Sedum *kamtschaticum*) ■ 4"–6" tall Summer; Zone 3–9; L, M–F

Turkish Speedwell (Veronica *liwanensis*) ■ 2" tall; Spring; Zone 4–8; L, F

Blue Star Creeper (Laurentia *fluviatilis*) ■ 3" tall; Late Spring–Summer; Zone 5/6–10; MO, M–F

Hardy Hummingbird Carpet (Zauschneria *arizonica*) 'Sky Island Orange' ■ Native; 30"–36" tall; Fall; Zone 5–9; N, M (not recommended for wet winters)

Hardy Plumbago (Ceratostigma *plumbaginoides*) ■ 6"–8" tall; Late Summer–Fall; Zone 5–9; L, M–F

Ground Covers for Part Shade to Shade

Bugleweed (Ajuga *reptans*) 'Toffee Chip' ■ 4"–6" tall; Spring; Zone 3–9; L–MO, S–M

Pennsylvania Sedge (Carex *pensylvanica*) ■ Native; 6"–12" tall; Early Summer; Zone 4–9; L, M

New Zealand Brass Buttons (Leptinella *squalida*) ■ 1"–2" tall; Spring; Zone 5–9; MO, M

Bunchberry (Cornus *canadensis*) ■ Native; 6" tall; Spring; Zone 2–7; N, M

Goldenstar (Chrysogonum *virginianum* var. *australe*) ■
Native; 6″ tall; Late Spring–Early Summer; Zone 5–8; L, M

Black Mondo Grass (Ophiopogon *planiscapus*
'Nigrescens') ■ 5″–6″ tall; Summer; Zone 5–10; N, S-M;

Barrenwort (Epimedium) 'Pretty in Pink' ■ 18″ tall;
Spring; Zone 4–8; N, M

European Wild Ginger (Asarum *europaeum*) ■ 6″ tall;
Spring; Zone 5–9; N, M

Colorful Pop-Ups

Spring, summer and fall blooming bulbs make vibrant embellishments to a living carpet. They magically "pop up," delight the eye, and then disappear until the following year. Assuming that most ground cover "rugs" tend to be short in nature, I'm recommending bulbs that flower at two feet or less; taller specimens seem awkwardly out of place. Plus, most of these stars are low- or no-deer browse and are hardy to at least Zone 6.

Spring blooming bulbs: Miniature Daffodils (Narcissus); species Kaufmanniana, Fosteriana and Greigii Tulips; Fritillaria; species Crocus; Puschkinia; Galanthus; dwarf Alliums; Eranthus and Leucojum.

Starflower (Triteleia 'Foxy')

Summer Blooming bulbs: the Pixie series of Asiatic Lilies; dwarf Oriental Lilies (i.e., 'Mona Lisa); Starflower (Triteleia); Summer Hyacinths (Galtonia *candicans*); and the POPSICLE series of Torch Lily (Kniphofia). Asiatic and Oriental Lilies are NOT deer resistant

Fall blooming bulbs: Colchicum; Autumn-blooming Crocus; Lycoris and Sternbergia *lutea*.

Autumn Daffodil (Sternbergia *lutea*)

Puschkinia *alba*

XERIC GARDENS

Parched. It's how many of us feel after working in the garden on a hot day. It is also the stressed condition of numerous landscapes in the United States. The Boston area and southern Maine (where I live) endured a dreadful drought in the summer of 2016. And we were not alone. Many parts of the country have had or are experiencing mild to extreme drought. To learn more, check out the website, http://droughtmonitor.unl.edu, which provides the degree of drought across the United States (updated weekly). As a result, many gardeners are embracing water-wise lessons learned from California's three-year record drought in 2012–2014.

This "firescape" garden, featuring pink Beardtongue (Penstemon) and silver Santolina, was designed by Owen Dell and Associates in California.

Xeriscaping is one popular solution to ever-increasing droughts. Gardens located in full sun and blasted with reflected heat are prime candidates. Add fast draining soil, slopes or windy locations to the mix and xeriscaping is a necessity!

Definitions, please!

Xeric, derived from the Greek word xeros, means dry.

Xeriscape, as defined by the Merriam-Webster dictionary, is "a landscaping method developed especially for arid and semiarid climates that utilizes water-conserving techniques (such as the use of drought-tolerant plants, mulch, and efficient irrigation)."

Perennials Calamintha and 'Silver Carpet' Lamb's Ears (Stachys *byzantina*) thrive in this sunny, rocky outcrop in NH.

Xeric gardening incorporates a number of strategies including plant selection, soil conditioning, mulch and watering methods. The more components you practice, the more drought resistant the garden, not to mention the money you will save on water bills.

Two of these thirst-quenching tactics can be achieved simultaneously:

■ **Mulching** Topdress the garden with nutrient-rich mulch such as leaf mold or shredded hardwood mixed with compost or manure. This organic material slowly breaks down into the soil, increasing its water-holding capacity as well as fertility. Mulch also reduces water evaporation from the garden's surface, maintains a more consistent soil temperature around plant roots, and minimizes weeds. Living mulches, such as creeping Thymes and Turkish Veronica, are also suitable options.

■ **Watering** The best practices are those that, 1) minimize water lost to evaporation, and 2) only wet targeted plants (i.e., not driveways, sidewalks, lawns). Efficient methods include soaker hoses, drip irrigation and possibly hand-watering. Even though xeric gardens need less water, you still need to provide consistent watering as plants get established and during extended periods of drought.

A drought tolerant meadow in Fall, featuring Asters, Switch Grass (Panicum) and False Blue Indigo (Baptisia). *Meadow designed by Linden L.A.N.D. Group.*

When researching plants, remember that a plant labeled as drought tolerant may do fine in New England but have an entirely different experience in Southern California. When scouting plants from the internet or gardening catalogs, it's best to double check the degree of drought tolerance with regional sources (i.e., cooperative extension office, local garden center). Similarly, a xeriscape garden in the Northeast will look different from one in the Southwest.

■ **Go native** Drought tolerant native plants are ideal, particularly ones suited for your area. An outstanding reference, mentioned earlier in this book, is the Native Plants Database (www.wildflower.org/collections), produced by The Lady Bird Johnson Wildflower Center. It lists native species by state. Another good site is soundnativeplants.com, which includes a native's growth rate (slow, moderate or fast).

GRAVEL GARDENS

Gravel gardens are a unique application of low-water landscaping. As with "generic" xeriscaping, minimal water consumption is essential. But gravel gardens – those mulched with a 1½- to 2-inch layer of gravel or pea stone – have their own particular requirements. Chanticleer Garden, located outside of Philadelphia, has one of the most breathtaking gravel gardens in the East. Lisa Roper, one of the garden's designers and caretakers, offers us some helpful tips for thriving gravel gardens.

"Sharp drainage is key," Roper says of her experience with Chanticleer's Gravel Garden. "To further accelerate drainage in our sandy soil, gravel or pea stone is used as a mulch to protect plant crowns from extended wetness." If your soil is not naturally fast draining, Roper suggests working one of these materials into the soil to open air and water channels: gravel, Rooflite (a product typically used for green roofs – a blend of porous lightweight aggregates such as expanded shale, blended with premium organic

The Gravel Garden at Chanticleer featuring yellow Bighead Knapweed (Centaurea *macrocephala*), peach Foxtail Lily (Eremurus) and White Lace Flower (Orlaya *grandiflora*).

matter), or Permatill (expanded shale with no organic matter). "Do not use organic matter," she warns, "it creates too rich a soil medium, causing plants to flop. Gravel garden plants do not appreciate rich soils or lots of fertilizer!" Another option for improving drainage is to garden on a slope.

In addition to highly porous soil, full sun is vital. Plants that thrive in gravel gardens (many of which hail from the Mediterranean) adore sun and heat. Chanticleer's Gravel Garden faces south and has no overhanging trees except a few upright Junipers.

About plant choices, Roper says, "I sort plants suitable for gravel gardens into two categories: 'reseeders' and 'plants that stay put.'" Gravel offers ideal conditions for many seeds to germinate, and there are some perennials that take full advantage of this. "Constant editing is needed to create balance," she notes. "Deadheading can help manage the amount of seeding, but I don't deadhead everything, for various reasons including: attractive seedheads, feed for birds (Coneflower), or if I want seedlings (i.e., short-lived Nasella)."

Some "enthusiastic" reseeders:

■ **Perennials:** Poppy Mallow (Callirhoe *involucrata*), Stipa grass (Nasella *tenuissima*), Donkeytail Spurge (Euphorbia *myrsinites*), Echinacea *tennesseensis*, Papaver *rupifragum* and Aster *oblongifolius* 'October Skies'.

■ **Annuals:** Larkspur, Orange California Poppy (Eschscholzia *californica*) and Minoan Lace (Orlaya *grandiflora*).

Moroccan Poppy (Papaver *rupifragum*)

Some "plants that stay put"
(with little or no reseeding):

Lavender, Butterfly Weed (Asclepias *tuberosa*), Lavender Cotton (Santolina *chamaecyparissus*), Russian Sage (Pervoskia), Sea Holly (Eryngium), 'Karl Foerster' Feather Reed Grass (Calamagrostis *acutiflora*), Silver Sage (Salvia *argentea*) and Artemesia 'Powis Castle'.

■ **Fertilizer?** Given their preference for dry, low-fertility soils, gravel gardens also save money on fertilizer and water. Roper fertilizes sparingly, only using liquid organic plant food as a boost to young or stressed plants. Regular watering is required after a garden is first planted in spring, but once established, no supplemental water is needed.

A final tip from Lisa Roper: "Gardening in hypertufa troughs is a simple way to start out small and try out gravel gardening. You can completely control the soil medium. Once you get a taste of how easy and rewarding gravel gardening is, you may become a huge fan like me."

A collection of hypertufa troughs in Chanticleer's Gravel Garden.

The steps in the Gravel Garden are ablaze with orange Butterfly Weed (Asclepias *tuberosa*), Larkspur and Nassella grass.

Purple Allium and Wisteria grace the morning landscape in this spring photo of the Gravel Garden.

The Gravel Garden still looks elegant even in late Fall.

THE RIGHT-SIZE MEADOW GARDEN

Picture a majestic meadow, overflowing with glorious grasses and wildflowers, alive with bees, birds and butterflies. It is nature's wonderland – a tapestry of living art unlike any other. A dynamic meadow inspires awe and a sense of well-being.

Unfortunately, this sweeping vista can be challenging to reproduce in urban settings, condominium developments or many residential neighborhoods. The "right-size meadow garden" is a miniature version of a meadow, better suited for smaller spaces. Equally important, a right-size meadow garden is more manageable for busy homeowners; plus, its refined appearance is more "socially acceptable" by finicky neighbors, especially when the garden is in the front yard.

Purple Coneflower, False Sunflower (Heliopsis), Phlox, Gayfeather (Liatris) and other native perennials make a breathtaking summer display. *Designed and installed by Rebecca Lindenmeyr of Linden L.A.N.D. Group*

■ **Bring in the wildflowers** In naturally occurring meadows, grasses compose the greatest percentage of plant material. A right-size meadow still relies on grasses but the ratio of grasses to wildflowers is reversed, with colorful, pollinator-friendly flowers playing a more dominate role. This minor modification can neutralize the occasional complaint that meadows can look unkempt and weedy. With careful selection of native wildflowers, a right-size meadow can be ablaze with vibrant flowers, spring through fall.

■ **A matter of scale** Another design difference with right-size meadows is the height of plants. Larger meadows can support natives like New York Ironweed that can soar to 8 feet in bloom. Smaller-scale meadows call for smaller specimens, usually 4 feet or shorter.

Large man-made meadows are usually planted with specialty seed mixes that contain both native grasses and wildflowers. This is far more economical than planting the expanse with containers or plugs. Although seeding is less expensive, it demands a greater time investment, including watering and weed management, especially in the first three years. Containers and plugs are more feasible for right-size meadows. The plants establish quickly and immediately start protecting exposed soil from weeds. Wildflower seeds can then be sown to fill in open channels between plants.

As you research plants for your right-size meadow, make sure they match the site's conditions: sunlight, soil type and moisture level, hardiness and heat zone. For the purpose of this right-size meadow illustration, I will be suggesting natives for full sun that are also drought tolerant. Please note, when I use the term "native," I am referring to plants that are native to North America. Resources for regional native plants include: The Lady Bird Johnson Wildflower Center's webpage, wildflower.org; Audubon Native Plants Database, Audubon.org/native-plants; and Ecoregional Planting Guides for Pollinators, http://pollinator.org/guides.

When coming up with this design concept for a miniaturized, flower-infused meadow, I interviewed my friend Rebecca Lindenmeyr, co-owner of Linden L.A.N.D. Group, located in Shelburne, VT. Until recently, she and her husband, Tim, operated this sustainable landscape and interior design company that served clients in Vermont, New York and New England. They have now decided to close the business and

A beautiful meadow that benefits both pollinators and the homeowner. *Designed by Rebecca Lindenmeyr of Linden L.A.N.D. Group*

The same meadow but later in the season, now bursting with purple asters and Black-Eyed Susans (Rudbeckia)

pursue new ventures. One of Rebecca's many gifts is creating breathtaking meadows. In addition to Rebecca's ideas shared in this section, other sources for learning about meadow gardens include *Garden Revolution,* by Larry Weaner and Thomas Christopher; *The American Meadow Garden,* by John Greenlee; Penn State Extensions article on natural meadows (extension.psu.edu/natural-resources/wildlife/landscaping-for-wildlife/pa-wildlife-5); and the Resources and Information page on Prairie Moon Nursery's website (prairiemoon.com), a nursery dedicated to North American native plants for restoration and gardening.

Caveat: Before planning and planting your "little meadow," research local ordinances and/or homeowner's associations to find out what rulings are in existence.

7 Steps to a Right-Size Meadow Garden

To create the most realistic looking right-size meadow, I suggest a space no smaller than 100 square feet (i.e., 5 feet wide by 20 feet long).

Let's start by going through steps for the site preparation.

■ **Step 1:** Locate an area on your property that gets full sun, a minimum of six hours of direct sunlight, and is well drained.

■ **Step 2:** Kill the existing grass by either solarization (see below) or spraying with an organic herbicide such as Phydura, Avenger or Burnout II (all OMRI approved). Do not remove the grass after it dies. It will serve as an organic mulch mat that slowly decomposes and keeps dormant weed seeds below it from germinating.

> **Solarization:** Mow the grass as short as possible, then cover it with clear 1–4 millimeter thick plastic (water the area first) or newspaper (see details in the section on living rugs). If you are using plastic, seal the edges with rocks or landscape staples. For best results, wait up to 6 months before removing the plastic if the area was weed infested.

■ **Step 3:** Cover the dead grass with a 3- to 5-inch layer of topsoil (the weed-free quality you would use for a vegetable or flower garden). Rake the soil level and then allow it to settle (eliminating air pockets) for a week or two. Sprinkling the leveled soil with water will help speed up the process.

■ **Step 4:** It's time to plant. Set out pots of "ground cover" grasses (grasses that shade the soil from incoming weed seeds), pollinator-friendly perennials, and taller ornamental grasses. Depending on the mature size of the potted plants, I recommend spacing pots approximately 18 inches apart. This will allow space for wildflower seeds that will be sown after the pots are installed.

■ **Step 5:** After the containers are planted, overseed open areas between plants with a regionally appropriate native seed mix composed of annuals (ideally reseeding varieties) and biennials. Follow packet instructions. The mix can also include perennials but this may require additional thinning of plants as the meadow matures. Look for mixes that are appropriate for your site conditions.

■ **Step 6:** Make sure to water the garden every few days (if there is no rain) for the first few weeks as container plants get established and seeds germinate. After this, once a week should be adequate. No mulch required.

■ **Step 7:** Be on the lookout for weeds that may blow into the garden as it is filling in. "Editing" will be an annual process as you thin out plants that may be "overly enthusiastic," add more of those you really like, or cast more wildflower seeds.

Swaths of Shasta Daisy and Pennslyvania Sedge (Carex *pensylvanica*) make a nice lawn alternative.

The Whitmire Wildflower Garden at Shaw Nature Reserve, a division of Missouri Botanical Garden.

The Plant Palette

Your right-size meadow will consist of weed-suppressing grasses, native wildflowers and taller ornamental grasses. Repeating fewer varieties throughout the bed is more natural looking than a wide assortment of plants polka-dotting the space. Use a natural meadow as your guide. To minimize weeding, at least 1/3 of the plants should be weed-suppressing grasses. Cool season grasses are best for weed control. These start actively growing in spring, shading exposed vulnerable soil from weed attacks, unlike warm season grasses that wait until early summer to take off.

Once you've created your plant list, check with the local garden center to see if they have the plants or can source them for you. If this is not an option, look into online nurseries. Rebecca Lindenmeyr highly recommends Prairie Moon Nursery. Unlike many nurseries, Prairie Moon sells plant trays comprised of 38 cells (5 inches deep by 2 inches wide). You can mix up to 6 varieties per tray.

Other recommended wildflower seed mix companies are Roundstone Native Seed (roundstoneseed.com); Ernst Seeds (ernstseed.com); and American Meadows (americanmeadows.com).

Suggested Drought-Tolerant Natives, Under 4 Feet Tall

NOTE: all are deer resistant, except for the Rudbeckia

4 Weed Suppressing Grasses

Prairie Dropseed (Sporobolous *heterolepis*) Sun; 2'–3' tall; Late Summer; Zone 3–8

Pennsylvania Sedge (Carex *pensylvanica*) Part Shade–Shade; 8" tall; Spring; Zone 3–8

Silky Thread Grass (Nassella (Stipa) *tenuissima*) Sun; 18" tall; Summer; Zone 7–10

Tufted Hairgrass (Deschampsia *cespitosa*) 'Goldtau' Part Sun–Part Shade; 12"–24" tall; Summer; Zone 4–9

Threadleaf Bluestar (Amsonia *hubrichtii*) ■ Sun; 3' tall; Spring; Zone; 4–9

Sundial Lupine (Lupinus *perennis*) ■ Sun–Part Shade; 1'–2' tall, Spring; Zone 4–8

Purple Coneflower (Echinacea *purpurea*) ■ Sun; 2'–3' tall; Summer; Zone 4–9; Also check other species, including *augustifolia, paradoxa, pallida* and *tennesseensis.*

Butterfly Weed (Asclepias *tuberosa*) ■ Sun; 18"–24" tall; Summer; Zone 3–9

Rudbeckia *subtomentosa* 'Little Henry' ▪ Sun–Part Sun; 3'–4' tall; Summer; Zone 4–8

Aster *oblongifolius* 'Raydon's Favorite' ▪ Sun; 2'–3' tall; Fall; Zone 3–8

Pink Hairgrass (Muhlenbergia *capillaris*) ▪ Sun–Part Sun; 2'–3' tall; Fall; Zone 6–10

Red Switch Grass (Panicum *virgatum*) PRAIRIE WINDS 'Cheyenne Sky' ▪ Sun; 3' tall; Fall; Zone 4–9

A 3-SEASON GARDEN TRIFECTA

For most of my life I lived near Saratoga Springs, NY, a city known in part for horse racing. Although not a gambler myself, I became familiar with betting lingo, including the prized Trifecta. To win the Trifecta (which can pay big dividends), one must correctly name the first, second and third place finishers.

Perennial Viola Bonnie Lassies 'Isabella' blooms from early spring until early fall; perennial Coreopsis var. 'Curry Up' blooms July through August; and annual Begonia *boliviensis* 'Bonfire' blooms spring until a hard frost. Photo taken in my garden.

I've come up with my own version of Trifecta for gardeners. The neat thing about this game is that it's simple to play, there are no rules and everybody wins! How can you say no?!

The goal of the game is to have an unbeatable, dazzling garden from spring through fall (even into winter). The playing field can be a landscape or container. All of the players (plants) must be low-maintenance and pollinator-friendly. The players are divided into three "starting gates": Spring, Summer and Fall. These gates represent a plant's peak bloom period, although as with great thoroughbreds, each plant has exceptional endurance, far surpassing other contestants for their blooming stamina, month after month. Each carefully selected contender has at least two seasons of interest provided by flowers, foliage, berries, seed heads and/or stem color. There are two tracks to choose from: one for sun-to-part-sun lovers and the other for shade-to-part-shade plants.

Before I go any further, I must confess the game is rigged. I've made sure every plant in this lineup is a winner. It is impossible not to have vibrant color, regardless of the combos that you pick. Each season includes a selection of perennials, flowering shrubs and ornamental grasses. Many are native to North America. In addition to these plants that should (remember that word *should*?) return year after year, there is another playing field just for award-winning annuals that provide non-stop color from either flowers (of course with no deadheading) and/or foliage. I also encourage placing bets (rigged to win) on long-lived, deer resistant bulbs that can be squeezed in between plant race horses.

The recommended game strategy is to pick at least one player from each "starting gate," setting up continuous bloom spring through fall. This will make both you and pollinators happy. That said, you may decide to only "play" summer and fall selections if you travel to a warmer climate in winter and don't get home until late spring. You can play the cards that fit your lifestyle – any way, you'll always win. Isn't this fun?

After you have selected your winning hand, it's time to decide on how many of each to purchase. The square footage of your landscape or container, as well as each plant's spacing recommendations, will be key factors. Unless your goal is for a formal look, I recommend that more than half of your picks

Perennial Amsonia *hubrechtii*, boxwood, and annual white Alyssum 'Snow Princess' are a winning combination in this Pittsburgh garden.

Solomon's Seal (Polygonatum *falcatum*) 'Nippon Sunbeam'

be planted in odd number groupings (i.e., 3, 5, 7). And don't worry your pretty little head about costs – I gave you plenty of money-saving shopping tips earlier in this book.

Okay, it is time to head off to the races with your winning ticket!

Trifecta Plant Lists

It was challenging to limit recommendations to only four plants per season, per light condition. It would be easier to give up chocolate. Each season includes perennials, annuals, ornamental grasses and flowering shrubs. Please also explore other plants within the featured plant families (genus). And remember that a plant listed for full sun may thrive in this situation in northern climates but require afternoon shade farther south.

PERENNIALS
Spring • Sun to Part Sun

Smooth Phlox (Phlox *glaberrima*) 'Triple Play' ■ Native; 12"–15" tall; Zone 4–8; flowers & foliage

False Indigo (Baptisia) DECADENCE 'Sparkling Sapphires' ■ Native; 2.5'–3' tall; Zone 4–9; flowers & seed pods

Arkansas Blue Star (Amsonia *hubrichtii*) ■ Native; 3' tall; Zone 4–9; flowers & fall foliage

Viburnum *nudum* 'Brandywine' ■ Native; 5'–6' tall; Zone 5–9; flowers & fall berries

Brunnera *macrophylla* 'Jack Frost' ■ 12"–15" tall; Zone 3–8; flowers & foliage

Dicentra *spectabilis* 'Gold Heart' ■ 30" tall; Zone 3–9; flowers & foliage

Hellebore x *ballardiae* 'HGC Spring Party' ■ 18" tall; Zone 5–8; flowers & foliage

Kalmia *latifolia* 'Minuet' ■ Native; 3' tall; Zone 5–9; flowers and evergreen foliage

Geranium 'Rozanne' ▪ 18"–20" tall; Zone 5–8; flowers for 8+ weeks

Coreopsis *verticillata* hybrid 'Show Stopper' ▪ 20" tall; Zone 5–9

Calamagrostis *acutiflora* 'Karl Foerster' ▪ Native; 5' tall; Zone 4–8

Physocarpus *opulifolius* 'Ginger Wine' ▪ Native; 5'–6' tall; Zone 3–7; flowers, foliage & exfoliating bark

**Astilbe *arendesii* 'Color Flash' ■ 18"–20" tall; Zone 4–8; flowers & foliage

Heucherella 'Pink Fizz' ■ 10"–13" tall; Zone 4–9; flowers & foliage

**Hakonechloa *macra* 'Aureola' ■ 12"–24" tall; Zone 5–9; foliage

**Hydrangea *arborescens* 'Haas Halo' ■ Native; 3'–5' tall; Zone 3–9; flowers & foliage

Vernonia *lettermania* 'Iron Butterfly' ■ Native; 30″–36″ tall; Zone 4–9; flowers & foliage

Sedum 'Night Embers' ■ 24″–26″ tall; Zone 3–9; flowers & foliage

Muhlenbergia *capillaris* ■ Native; 2′-3′ tall; Zone 6–10; flowers & foliage

Caryopteris *incana* 'Sunshine Blue II' ■ 24″–36″ tall; Zone 5–9; flowers & foliage

Kirengeshoma *palmata* ■ 3'–4' tall; Zone 5–8; flowers & foliage

Tricyrtis *formosana* 'Autumn Glow' ■ 24"–26" tall; Zone (4)5–9; flowers & foliage

Actaea *ramosa* (formerly Cimicifuga) ■ Native; 'Hillside Black Beauty' 3' tall (up to 5' in flower); Zone 4–8; flowers & foliage

Hamamelis *virginiana* 'Little Suzie' ■ Native; 4'–5' tall; Zone 3–8; flowers & foliage

ANNUALS
Sun to Part Sun

Supertunia Vista 'Bubblegum' ■ 12″ mounds, trails up to 36″; no deadheading

Lobularia 'Snow Princess' ■ 4″–8″ mounds, trails to 24″; no deadheading

Lantana 'Luscious Marmalade' ■ 12″–18″ tall; no deadheading

Angelonia ANGELFACE 'Perfectly Pink' ■ 18″–30″ tall; no deadheading

Part Shade to Shade

Torenia SUMMER WAVE 'Large Blue' ■ 8"–10" mounds, trails up to 36"; no deadheading

New Guinea Impatiens (Impatiens *hawkeri***)** INFINITY 'Electric Cherry' 10"–14" tall; no deadheading

Begonia *benariensis* (BIG series) ■ 12"–18" tall; no deadheading

Browallia ENDLESS 'Illumination' ■ 12"–16" tall; no deadheading

Note: For more cultural information, as well as additional pictures of these supreme plant recommendations – and others in this book – please check out the following websites:

americanmeadows.com
anniesannuals.com
bluestoneperennials.com
brokenarrownursery.com
brushwoodnursery.com
gardencrossings.com
highcountrygardens.com
lazyssfarm.com
missouribotanicalgarden.org
monrovia.com
nearlynativenursery.com
nhhostas.com
perennialresource.com
plantdelights.com
prairiemoon.com
provenwinners.com
springmeadownursery.com
sunnyborder.com
waltersgardens.com ■

REGAL CONTAINERS ON A DOLLAR-STORE BUDGET

*C*ontainer gardening continues its upward popularity trend. This is no surprise when one takes into account that the two largest demographic age groups in the United States are Baby Boomers (ages 53–71) and Millennials (ages 20–36) – as of 2017, per the U.S. Census Bureau. The former are downsizing and the latter, who now outnumber the Boomers, are increasingly choosing to live in urban settings.

Combine the gardening needs of aging Boomers (like me) who are right-sizing, with fast-paced, city-dwelling Millennials (like my son in NYC), and container gardening is an ideal solution.

My son and I celebrating Christmas 2016 in NYC

These attractive self-watering planters from Gardener's Supply Company can go a full week, or more, without watering.

But I Thought Container Gardening was More Work!

It used to be – when container gardening meant being a slave to daily watering. I know that drudgery well. For years I would lug heavy watering cans and drag kinking hoses around my property.

Thank heavens for self-watering pots! This time-saving technology has revolutionized the gardening industry. Now state-of-the-art, self-watering pots are decidedly easier to use than irrigating most gardens. Plus, these "smart" systems are extremely water-wise, reducing precious water lost to evaporation, and at the same time reducing untimely plant deaths due to over- or under-watering. Plants "know" when they are thirsty and draw water as needed from a reservoir in the container's base. Capillary action then delivers water into the potting soil, keeping planters consistently moist. Your only job is to periodically check the water level indicator and refill the tank when needed. Another perk of many systems is that water-soluble fertilizer can be added to the reservoir, eliminating fertilizer runoff.

Gardening in containers offers the timeless satisfaction of growing one's own flowers and food, but also allows for limited space, time and physical ability. Another dividend is cost-effectiveness. New container technology has resulted in lower water usage, as well as stylish weather-resistant pots for overwintering plants. Spending money wisely appeals to everyone, from Boomers on retirement budgets to Millennials, many of whom are saddled with college loans and home mortgages.

More Good Reasons to Garden in Containers:

- Fewer weeds
- Reduced disease and insect problems as well as damage from chewing pests (i.e., slugs, deer, rabbits)
- Easier to create healthy, plant-thriving soil conditions
- The "silver bullet" if you have impenetrable soil caused by tree and shrub roots
- Easier accessibility for physically challenged gardeners
- Harder accessibility for pets that "disrespect" garden boundaries

Planters double as nature's "duct tape." Containers make quick fixes of landscape problems:

- They conceal eyesores (i.e., air conditioning units, electrical meters, generators, neighbors).
- They occupy space where spring blooming bulbs, bleeding hearts or ephemerals have died back.
- They restrain aggressive roots of eye-catching perennials or suckering flowering shrubs.
- They infuse striking focal points in spaces lacking color.

If you were not already a fan of container gardening, I hope I've piqued your interest!

This fabulous urn welcomes visitors to Avant Gardens, a unique garden center and design company in Dartmouth, MA.

But given this book's money- and time-saving theme, suitable containers should have many, if not all, of the following features:

■ **Superior quality and durability**

■ **Self-watering.** The advancements in watering systems for both outdoor and indoor planters have been unparalleled. For example, the TruDrop Watering System in the Crescent line of pots, can store between two and six weeks of water without refilling!

A Crescent pot with the TruDrop Watering System

Planter Plethora

Container choices are limitless. Commercially produced pots can be made from a huge assortment of materials including wood, concrete, metal, plastic, terra-cotta and resin. Pots come in all sizes, shapes and colors. Recycling and repurposed vessels are the rage. It can be fascinating, and sometimes bewildering, to see what people come up with.

An ingenious way to grow an herb "garden" in a small space.

■ **Stylish.** A stylish container has functionality that can also double as art, or create a unique focal point.

■ **Lightweight and mobile.** Pots need to be easily maneuvered to suit changing needs: provide privacy, block intense afternoon sun, or open up additional entertainment space. Rolling planters with built-in casters (wheels) are fashionable and highly functional.

■ **Space efficient.** Gardening in small spaces makes every inch of living area prime real estate. Containers modified for walls, railings, roofs and ceilings are an additional asset.

■ **All-weather resistant.** Containers that can remain outside year round are especially appreciated in colder climates (Zones 7 or colder). Attractive planters can contain winter-hardy plants, including evergreens, or be decorated with greenery and holiday décor. Light-weight, winter-tough containers are typically made out of resin, foam, fiberglass, aluminum or stainless steel. Be sure there is a drainage hole in the base. It there isn't one, make one by using a drill with the appropriate bit (bits will vary based on the pot's material). IF you really must have terra-cotta pots (which typically crack with freezing and thawing temperatures) then borrow Ray Mims' technique. Mims, the former director of horticulture at the Denver Botanic Gardens (in Zone 4), paints the interior of his pots with pool paint, sealing the porous surface so that moisture doesn't enter.

Sources For Bargain Basement Prices

- Fall sales at garden centers
- Ocean State Job Lot, Big Lots, and similar venues
- Christmas Tree Shops
- Thrift and consignment stores
- Yard sales
- Good Will, ReStore (Habitat for Humanity shops)
- Home goods stores like Costco, Ikea, Home Depot, Lowes, Walmart, Target
- Craig's List, Overstock.com, Groupon

Fill 'er Up!

High quality potting medium is essential for successful container gardening, just as healthy soil is the foundation for thriving flower and vegetable gardens. Topnotch mixes provide good aeration and drainage for roots.

■ **About soilless mixes** – Soilless mixes contain no garden soil, eliminating the problem of soil-borne diseases. Most soilless mediums contain a combination of peat moss (or coconut coir), perlite, vermiculite and sand (or bark). You can buy this by the bag or make your own, which is a lot cheaper. There are numerous recipes available on the internet, including those provided by many cooperative extension offices.

While soilless mixes are essential when growing plants from seed, are they also essential in flower planters? Many would say yes. I disagree, especially for vessels that also contain perennials,

shrubs or conifers. Many gardeners, including myself, will add compost, and sometimes soil as well, to the "mixing bowl." But I never use soil alone in containers, as this leads to problems with aeration and drainage.

I have found success with the following homemade recipe for containers that are NOT self-watering:

> 2 parts soilless mix
> (like Espoma's Organic Potting Mix)
>
> I part soil (sandy loam, not clay)
>
> I part compost or leaf mold

Note: Self-watering containers require lighter potting blends that enhance capillary action for wicking moisture from the water reservoir. You can purchase products especially designed for self-watering containers or play "soil chef" and whip up your own masterpiece. If you use a recipe from the internet, make sure that soil is not one of the ingredients. I use the above recipe for self-watering containers as well, but I eliminate the soil.

KEEP THE CASH IN YOUR POCKET!

Don't throw money away by buying potting mixes that include fertilizer, especially time-released products. It is cheaper to apply a granular, slow-release organic fertilizer around each plant after positioning it in the container. It makes no sense to use fertilizer-laced potting soil when much of the material is not even close to the roots!

Don't waste money on potting soil that includes hydro-gels (also called water-retentive crystals). There is now research that questions the safety of these gels, as well as the actual effectiveness.

I filled this container 2/3 full with crushed plastic pots and then placed landscape fabric over the "filler" before scooping in potting soil.

Cut the amount of potting soil you need. Have a large planter? Use this trick. For large planters that are NOT self-watering, slash the amount of potting soil required by filling half (or two-thirds) of the space with "filler."

Filler suggestions:

- packing peanuts (as long as they are not made from corn starch)
- pine cones
- bubble wrap
- milk jugs
- soda bottles
- crushed annual 6-packs

Pack these into the container and then cut a piece of landscape fabric or screening to place on top of the "fill." Finish by scooping in potting soil to within an inch of the rim.

■ **Can I re-use last year's potting soil?** Recycle potting soil from flower containers or window boxes – but only if the previous plants were disease free. If you notice salt buildup (tiny white crystals) on the surface, discard the top one or two inches before storing the remainder. Even though some gardeners reuse the same material for several years, I like to recharge my recycled medium with 25% fresh potting soil each spring. You can also recycle older potting soil in the garden or compost pile.

Unloading bulk material from the back of a truck was never easier using a Loadhandler (Loadhandler.com).

Save in Bulk

■ **Potting soil.** Buy potting soil by the cubic yard (bulk) instead of by the bag. Purchasing material by the cubic yard not only saves money, it's also environmentally friendly (eliminating extra plastic bags). Check this out: a cubic yard of potting soil equals 27 cubic-foot bags sold at garden centers. The average price for a cubic yard of potting soil in my area is approximately $145. The average price of one bag of similar material is $8.99; 27 bags is $242.73. That's almost a $100 savings! One cubic yard easily fits into the back of a pickup truck. Why not get a few neighbors to pitch in for a yard (or the neighborhood association)? Google "potting soil by the cubic yard" to find possible suppliers in your region.

■ **Topsoil, compost and mulch.** The same dollar-saving philosophy applies to bulk orders of topsoil, compost and mulch, but these are far less expensive (usually under $50 per cubic yard, depending on the material). Many people have the false impression that one cubic yard is a lot more than it really is. Perhaps this will help you visualize a cubic yard: the typical garden variety wheelbarrow holds three cubic feet, so it would take nine wheelbarrows to equal one cubic yard. Here is a simple formula for calculating the quantity needed for a project: one cubic yard covers 100 square feet approximately 3 inches deep.

AXE THE ANNUALS

I think it is safe to say that most ornamental planters include a majority, if not all, annuals. Annuals require a yearly investment of money, as well as time needed to keep replanting them. Doesn't it make sense to change this absurd seasonal practice?

Instead of filling containers with mostly annuals, replace at least half (or more) with hardy perennials and woody plants. Not only will you pocket more of your hard-earned money, but the investment typically "compounds" to yield more plants! Many perennials can be divided in spring. The abundance can then be planted in additional containers, gardens or shared with friends.

My 6 Criteria for Container-worthy Perennials, Flowering Shrubs and Conifers.

They must be:

1. **Cold Qualified.** Plants overwintered in outdoor containers need to be at least two hardiness zones colder than the local zone.
2. **Beauty Queens.** Winning choices should have an exceptional long season of interest with impeccable form.
3. **Polite.** Slow-spreading, non-thuggish plants make good bed partners.
4. **Thirstless.** Well, not really thirstless, but drought tolerance is important.

5. **Restrained.** Plants with smaller root systems are better adapted for confined spaces.
6. **Slender.** Narrow girths are prized for combo containers. Excessively wide plants outgrow their welcome.

Designing with Thrillers, Fillers and Spillers (without annuals)

I'll be making hardy plant recommendations based on the role that annuals fill in a container design. The standard design "mantra" for containers calls for thrillers, fillers and spillers. Thrillers are showboats – commanding attention; providing height and a strong vertical element. Fillers dance around the thriller and are typically more rounded or mounded in form. And spillers "live on the edge," trailing gracefully over the rim and down the side. When creating your masterpiece, be sure that all "performers" dance to the same beat (i.e., sunlight, moisture and fertilizer requirements).

I planted my light-weight, self-watering Viva container with mostly perennials – Hosta, Coral Bells 'Lava Lamp', Hakone Grass 'All Gold', Creeping Yellow Jenny and Bugleweed 'Pink Lightning'.

Perennial and Woody Thrillers

Juniper *communis* 'Compressa' ■ Sun; 2'–6' tall, 1'–1.5' wide; Zone 3–6; evergreen; deer resistant

Bushel & Berry 'Jelly Bean' Blueberry ■ Sun; 1'–2' tall; Spring flowers; Summer fruit; Fall foliage; Zone 4–8

Hydrangea *paniculata* 'Dharuma' ■ Sun–Part Shade; 4' tall; Summer; Zone 3–8

Witch-Hazel (Hamamelis *vernalis*) 'Quasimodo' ■ Sun–Part Shade; 3'–4' tall; Spring fragrant flowers, Fall foliage; Zone 4–8; deer resistant

Perennial and Woody Thrillers

Butterfly Bush (Buddleia) Lo & Behold 'Pink Micro Chip'
■ Sun; 18"–24" tall; Summer; Zone 5–9; deer resistant

Japanese Blood Grass (Imperata *cylindrica*) 'Red Baron'
■ Sun–Part Sun; 12"–18" tall; Zone 5–9; deer resistant

Sedum 'Maestro' ■ Sun; 24"–30" tall; Fall; Zone 3–9

Peruvian Lily (Alstroemeria) 'Inca Joli' ■ Sun–Part Sun;
16"–20" tall; Summer; Zone (5) 6–9

Perennial Fillers

Foamy Bells (Heucherella) FUN AND GAMES 'Red Rover'
■ Sun–Shade; 6"–8" foliage mounds; Spring; Zone 4–9

Coral Bells (Heuchera) DOLCE 'Silver Gumdrop' ■
Sun–Shade; 6"–8" foliage mounds; Summer; Zone 4–9;
deer resistant

Threadleaf Coreopsis 'Red Elf' ■ Sun; 8"–12" Summer–
Early Fall; Zone 5–9; deer resistant

Hen & Chicks (Sempervivum) CHICK CHARMS 'Gold
Nugget' ■ Sun; 2"–3" mounds; Late Summer; Zone 9

Perennial Fillers

Sedge (Carex *siderosticha*) 'Banana Boat' ∎
Part Shade–Shade; 6"–12" tall; Late Spring; Zone 5–9

Bellflower (Campanula *carpatica*) 'Rapido White' ∎
Sun–Part Sun; 5"–7" tall; Summer; Zone 3–8

Pinks (Dianthus) 'Paint the Town Fuchsia' ∎
Sun–Part Sun; 6"–8" tall; Spring; Zone 4–9

Black Mondo Grass (Ophiopogon *planiscapus*)
'Nigrescens' ∎ Part Sun–Part Shade; 5"–6" tall;
Summer; Zone 5–10

Hakone Grass (Hakonechloa *macra*) 'Aureola' (Japanese Hakone Grass) ■ Part Sun–Shade; 1'–2' cascading; Zone 5–9; deer resistant

Creeping Yellow Jenny (Lysimachia *nummularia*) 'Aurea' ■ Sun–Part Sun; 2"–4" tall; Zone 3–9

Bugleweed (Ajuga *reptans*) 'Pink Lightning' ■ Sun–Shade; 4"–6" tall; Spring; Zone 3–8; deer resistant

Serbian Bellflower (Campanula *poscharskyana*) 'Blue Waterfall' ■ Sun–Part Shade; 8"–10" tall; Summer; Zone 4–9

Perennial Spillers

Creeping Sedum (Sedum *spurium*) 'Fulda Glow' ■ Sun; 3"–4" tall; Late Summer; Zone 3–9

Clematis 'Fleuri' ■ Sun–Part Shade; 3'–4' stems; Summer; Zone 4–9; deer resistant

Poppy Mallow (Callirhoe *involucrata*) ■ Sun; 5" tall; long trailing, flower-covered stems; Summer; Zone 4–9

Hardy Ice Plant (Delosperma) 'Lavender Ice' ■ Sun; 2"–4" tall; Summer; Zone 4–9; deer resistant

Perennial Plant List for a Sun to Part Sun Container Design

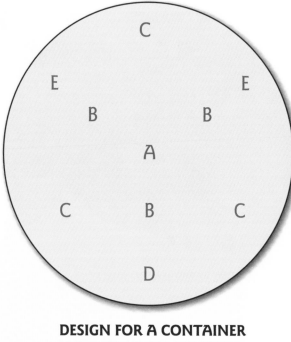

**DESIGN FOR A CONTAINER
VIEWED FROM ALL SIDES**

A = Anise Hyssop (Agastache *aurantiaca*) 'Apricot Sprite'
    18" tall; Summer; Zone 6–9; deer resistant

B = Coral Bells (Heuchera) DOLCE 'Cinnamon Curls' ■
    8" mounds; Spring, early Summer; Zone 4–9;
    deer resistant

C = Creeping Yellow Jenny (Lysimachia *nummularia*) 'Aurea'
    2"–4" tall; Zone 3–9

D = Oregano (Origanum) 'Kent Beauty' ■ 6"–8" (trailing);
    Summer; Zone 6–9; deer resistant

E = Serbian Bellflower (Campanula *poscharskyana*)
    'Blue Waterfall' ■ 8"–10" tall; Summer; Zone 4–9

A

B

C

D

E

Perennial Plant List for Part Shade to Shade Container Design

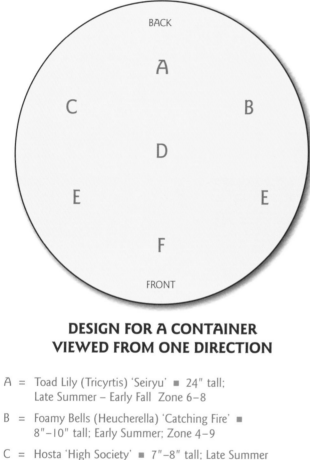

BACK

A

C   B

D

E   E

F

FRONT

DESIGN FOR A CONTAINER
VIEWED FROM ONE DIRECTION

A = Toad Lily (Tricyrtis) 'Seiryu' ■ 24" tall;
Late Summer – Early Fall Zone 6–8

B = Foamy Bells (Heucherella) 'Catching Fire' ■
8"–10" tall; Early Summer; Zone 4–9

C = Hosta 'High Society' ■ 7"–8" tall; Late Summer
(pale lavender flowers); Zone 3–9

D = Black Mondo Grass (Ophiopogon *planiscapus*)
'Nigrescens' ■ 5"–6" tall; Summer; Zone 5–10

E = Bugleweed (Ajuga *reptans*) 'Toffee Chip' ■
4"–6" (trailing); Spring; Zone 4–9; deer resistant

F = Plumbago (Ceratostigma *plumbaginoides*) ■ 8"–12"
(trailing); Late Summer–Fall; Zone 5–9; deer resistant

A

B

C   D

E   F

WINTER STORAGE

Now that you've made the decision to replace many "short-lived relationships" (annuals) with "long-term commitments" (perennials and woody plants), the next step is to provide for their winter accommodations. For those of you in hardiness Zones 7 or warmer, you probably rarely, if ever, experience hard freezes, so for you this section is just for giggles.

Overwinter hardy plants (perennials, deciduous shrubs and trees) in the following three ways:

1. **In the same container they've been growing in.** Continue watering the plants until they are dormant. You can leave the container outside in the winter elements IF plants are hardy to at least two zones colder than where you live AND the vessel is weather-resistant. If you're

My mophead Hydrangeas (Hydrangea *macrophylla*) wintering over in my unheated garage. I took this photo in late March when the shrubs were starting to "wake-up" from their winter nap.

Here are the same Hydrangeas on July 3 in their full glory!

Here is my "storage closet" with plants that I divided from my garden as well as others purchased at fall sales.

not using the container as a winter focal point, then store it close to the foundation of your home (east or north side), out of the path of winter winds. If the container is too heavy (or unwieldy) to be relocated and is sited in the open, then protect "sleeping beauties" from water or ice build-up by either slightly tipping the vessel to allow run-off or covering the planter with a tarp. Finally, if additional protection makes *you* feel better, wrap containers in bubble wrap, tarp, foam or a "blankie."

Note: IF the container is not weather resistant and/or the plants are only cold hardy to your zone *(if that)*, then stow the planter in an unheated garage, shed or barn.

This is my solution for growing lush, flowering bigleaf Hydrangeas (Hydrangea *macrophylla*) in Zone 5. All Hydrangeas in this group (mophead or lacecap) form their flower buds in late summer or early fall. These buds are susceptible to winter kill. Extreme cold temperatures (i.e., below zero), bitter wind-chills, little snow, or widely fluctuating winter temperatures (a warm spell followed by a cold snap) can have devastating effects. My Hydrangeas are not subjected to this abuse anymore. I grow them in containers and overwinter them in my unheated garage. After the Hydrangeas go dormant in late fall (dropping all of their leaves), I relocate them to the garage (or my sister's barn).

2. **In recycled plastic nursery pots.** Remove plants from the planter and place in plastic pots filled with potting soil. The larger the pot, the better insulated the roots will be. Water pots until plants go dormant. Pots can be stored together outside under a tarp along the east or north side of a building IF the plants are hardy to at least your hardiness zone. Mulch, leaves or straw can be tucked around and over the containers for additional insulation before applying the tarp. If gnawing mice, voles, chipmunks or squirrels are a problem, protect vulnerable roots by first placing chicken wire or screening over the pots before layering material and covering with a tarp.

If plants are only borderline hardy, then store pots inside an unheated shed, barn or garage. Don't fret if the interior experiences freezing temperatures, unless inside temperatures drop below 10° F, which is unlikely. If it gets that cold inside, it's survival of the fittest!

3. **In the ground.** Remove plants from the container and dig them into a flower garden (perhaps where annuals were), vegetable bed or holding area (housing all those plants that you've bought but haven't figured out where to put them).

Overwintering Evergreens

Evergreens do not go dormant in winter; they still need sunlight (for photosynthesis) and water. If needed, water plants during the day when temperatures are above freezing. Make sure the container is not exposed to winter winds that can desiccate (dry out) leaves and needles. An application of Wilt-Pruf may be helpful for reducing water loss, as well as damage from wind or sun burn.

CONTAINER WITHIN A CONTAINER

Some plants are irresistible when in flower, but then spiral into an ugly mess a few weeks later. Take spring-blooming bulbs for example: Their blossoms are exquisite, chasing away the winter blues and promising good things ahead. But then the dying, ratty foliage (that usually lasts longer than the flowers) is a downer.

One solution is to grow bulbs in a container within a larger container. Once the flowers start to fade, simply remove the container and slide a different plant in its place; perhaps a colorful, non-stop flowering annual. Presto! Then plant the container of bulbs somewhere out of sight where it can gracefully die back out of view. Come fall, if the ornamental container is weather resistant, you can replace the annual with the pot of dormant bulbs. You could also wait until spring to lift the pot out of the ground, insert into a container and enjoy another spirit-lifting show. You can do the same with other spring-flowering "sprinters": primrose, dwarf Oriental poppies, English Daisy (Bellis *perennis*) and lovely ephemerals such as Bloodroot (Sanguinaria *canadensis*) and Shooting Star (*Dodecatheon*).

The same design trick works with summer-flowering bulbs that have "good and bad" sides. Candidates include shorter varieties of Asiatic, Oriental and Orienpet Lilies.

Award-winning designer Deborah Trickett, owner of The Captured Garden, plants spring-blooming bulbs with perennials and annuals.

Sleight-of-hand for indoor planters, too!

Use the same technique for eye-popping planters that shine year-round – indoors and out. Create the foundation composition with showy foliage plants (many can be houseplants). Leave a space for "the magic act." For instance, the outdoor "space-holder" might be one of the following long-blooming, compact annuals that need no deadheading:

Browallia
Double Impatiens
Dwarf upright Fushcia like 'Tom Thumb'
Wax Begonia
Million Bells (Calibrachoa)
Or how about a micro-mini rose that only
gets 6 to 12 inches tall?

When cooler temperatures approach, swap the
"outdoor resident" for the indoor flower-star that
will bloom a good part of the winter. Remember
when selecting plants to make sure that they
share similar growing conditions. Possibilities
include:

Cape Primrose (Streptocarpus)
Dwarf Crown of Thorns 'Spendens'
Sinningia 'Prudence Risley'
Kalanchoe ■

Dwarf Crown of Thorns 'Spendens' blooms month after month!

Sinningia 'Prudence Risley' never fails to draw attention with its prolific blooming habit.

ON TO "GREENER" PASTURES

*C*ongratulations! You have completed the Academy of Shrewd Plant Hunters training program. You are primed to detect the sweetest deals and sidestep money-losing minefields. You're also equipped to make smart plant and design choices, adding beauty and value to your landscape while being a worthy steward of the planet.

And now what are you going to do with all the money you save and the free time you'll have with less garden maintenance? Perhaps explore new hobbies like bird watching, bee keeping or travelling? Maybe you could volunteer at a local nonprofit? More time with loved ones and friends is always a good choice.

Whatever it is, I hope you will also share your gardening passion with others, especially our youth and elderly.

Warm Wishes,

Kerry Ann (and Zoe)

INDEX

INDEX

Photo Credits

Photo Credits

Photo Credits

ACKNOWLEDGMENTS

My thanks go to so many people who inspired and supported me in writing this fourth gardening book. First to God, "who is able to do exceedingly, abundantly more than we can ask or think." And to my patient husband, Sergio, who was always there to encourage me and tirelessly edit my writing. I am also deeply thankful to a special team of enthusiastic cheerleaders: my son, Evan; my sisters, Kim and Jane; and Dad and my stepmom, Carol.

I also could not have written the book without the generosity of so many that provided images and advice: Proven Winners; Walters Gardens; Spring Meadow Nursery; Terra Nova Nurseries; Monrovia; Sunny Border Nurseries; Bluestone Perennials; Classy Groundcovers; North Creek Nurseries; Missouri Botanical Gardens; Deborah Trickett, owner of The Captured Garden; Lisa Roper at Chanticleer Garden; Rebecca Lindenmeyr of Linden L.A.N.D. Group; Brushwood Nursery and many others. My friends at Estabrook's Nursery were saints to allow me access to their inventory to use for photo props, including the book's cover.

And where would I be without the amazing team at St. Lynn's Press: Paul Kelly, Cathy Dees, Holly Rosborough and Chloe Wertz. Thank you for the pleasure of writing this book together.

As this writing journey comes to a close, I stand amazed at the new friends I've made, the lessons learned, the never-ending support of my family, and the deep, heartfelt satisfaction of having accomplished another book. Who would have dreamed it? Not me! ■

ABOUT THE AUTHOR

𝒦erry Ann Mendez is dedicated to teaching the art of low-maintenance flower gardening and landscaping to gardeners of all ages and abilities. As a garden consultant, designer, writer and lecturer, she focuses on time-saving gardening techniques and workhorse plant material, as well as organic and sustainable practices.

She has been featured in numerous magazines, including *Horticulture, Fine Gardening, Garden Gate* and *Better Homes and Gardens' Garden Ideas & Outdoor Living,* and has been a monthly columnist for *518Life, Capital Region Living* and *Today's Garden Center* magazines. Recently, she was awarded the Massachusetts Horticultural Society's Gold Medal, an honor given to outstanding horticulturalists, plant innovators, and those who have made significant contributions to the enjoyment and appreciation of plants and the environment.

Kerry Ann is a "passionate perennialist" who enjoys mixing humor with practical information. Her previous books include *The Right-Size Flower Garden* (2015, St. Lynn's Press), *The Ultimate Flower Gardener's Top Ten Lists* and *Top Ten Lists for Beautiful Shade Gardens – Seeing Your Way Out of the Dark.* She is a sought-after speaker, giving over 100 presentations annually, nationwide. Through her business, Perennially Yours, she has conducted more than 1,000 home garden and landscape consultations, and works seasonally at independent garden centers. Kerry Ann produced seven national gardening webinars for Horticulture that were among the best attended of all their webinar offerings, and now produces her own popular gardening webinars.

A ongtime resident of Upstate New York, Kerry Ann now resides in Kennebunk, Maine, with her husband, Sergio. Their son, Evan Christian, is working in New York City and enjoying the 'city that never sleeps'. For more about Kerry Ann and Perennially Yours, visit www.pyours.com. ∎

OTHER BOOKS FROM ST. LYNN'S PRESS

www.stlynnspress.com

The Right-Size Flower Garden
by Kerry Ann Mendez
192 pages • Hardback
ISBN: 978-0989268875

The Foodscape Revolution
by Brie Arthur
192 pages • Hardback
ISBN: 978-1943366187

The Spirit of Stone
by Jan Johnsen
192 pages, Hardback
ISBN: 978-1943366194

The Monarch
by Kylee Baumle
160 pages, Hardback
ISBN: 978-1943366170